PAST INTO PRESENT 3

1700 – Present Day

PAST INTO PRESENT 3

1700 – Present Day

Peter Fisher

Nicholas Williams

Series Editor:
Martin Booth

COLLINS
EDUCATIONAL

COLLINS LOWER SCHOOL HISTORY

CONTENTS

The Industrial Revolution

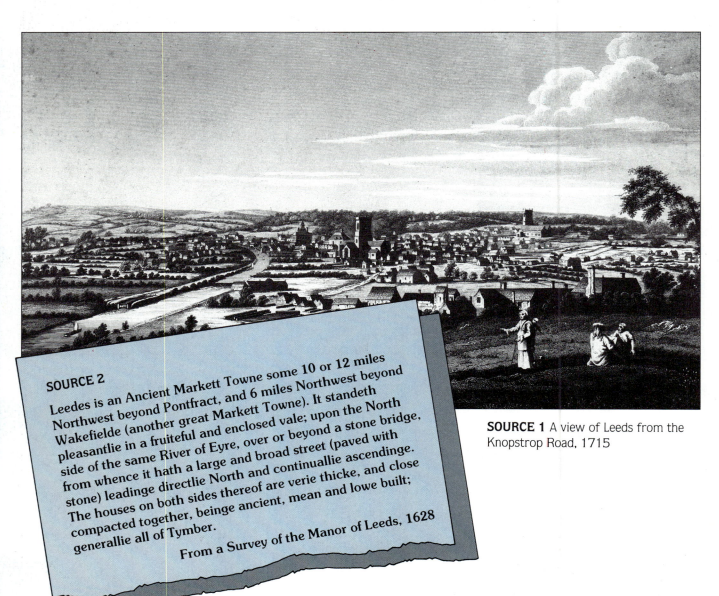

SOURCE 1 A view of Leeds from the Knopstrop Road, 1715

SOURCE 3 A view of Leeds, 1858

SOURCE 4

Leeds is situated on a slope running down towards the River Aire, which meanders about a mile and a half through the town, and is liable to overflow during thaws or heavy rains. The higher or western districts are clean for so large a town, but the lower parts contiguous [next to] the river and its becks or rivulets are dirty, confined, and, in themselves, sufficient to shorten life, especially infant life; add to this the disgusting state of the lower parts of the town about Kirk-gate, March-lane, Cross-street, and Richmond-road, principally owing to a general want [lack] of paving and draining, irregularity of building, the abundance of courts and blind alleys, as well as the almost total absence of the commonest means of promoting cleanliness, and we have then quite sufficient data to account for the surplus mortality [deaths] in these unhappy regions of filth and misery.

The Artizan, *1843*

LEEDS WAS ONCE a pleasant market town (Sources 1 and 2). By the mid-nineteenth century it was a squalid and overcrowded city (Sources 3 and 4). This complete change was a consequence of the Industrial Revolution.

---

1 **Using Sources 1 to 4, make a list of all the ways in which Leeds changed between 1628 and the mid-nineteenth century.**

2 **What is the most noticeable change?**

AIMS

Leeds changed from a pleasant market town to an overcrowded city because of the growth of factories during the Industrial Revolution.

This unit looks at the development of factories and, in particular, the part played by the first factory owners. You will be able to put yourself in the place of these men. You will be asked to make some of the difficult decisions they made. You will be developing your EMPATHY* skills, that is, your ability to understand the motives and actions of these early factory owners and to see things from their point of view.

Looking back, it is easy to criticise the many mistakes the first factory owners made; it is easy to misunderstand the part they played. You will have the opportunity to see if you can do any better. You might decide that historians should not judge past events and characters by present-day standards but only by the standards of the time.

This chapter is also concerned with continuity. This is the idea that the present and the future are very much the result of what happened in the past. Changes which began with the growth of the factories during the Industrial Revolution still very much shape the society we live in today.

* Words printed in SMALL CAPITALS are explained in the Glossary on page 155.

THE FIRST FACTORIES

Until the mid-eighteenth century most people in Britain lived in villages or small towns. Most of them earned their living from the land. The largest industry was the woollen cloth industry. All the spinning, weaving and dyeing was carried out in cottages by small groups of workmen and their families (see Sources 5 and 6).

Compare the written source (Source 5) with the picture (Source 6). How do they agree or disagree?

From the 1760s onwards, new inventions made it possible for spinning and weaving to be done in factories. One of the most important new machines was Richard Arkwright's 'water frame' (Source 7). This was a spinning machine that produced a strong, coarse thread.

As you can see from Source 7, the early version of this machine was certainly small enough to fit in a cottage. Arkwright was a clever businessman, though. He hoped to make a fortune out of his invention. He took out a patent on the water frame to stop other people copying it. Now the machine could only be used in his own factories or in the factories of other businessmen who were prepared to pay him for using it.

Also, the water frame was designed to be driven by water power. It did not make sense to erect a waterwheel to power just one machine in a cottage. Far better to build a factory, where one waterwheel could drive several machines.

Source 8 is a contemporary portrait of Richard Arkwright. It makes him look very jolly and kindly. Yet Matthew Boulton, a factory owner who knew Arkwright well, described him as a tyrant. On Arkwright's death, a magazine wrote that his 'frugality [carefulness with money] bordered very nearly on parsimony [stinginess]'. In other words, Arkwright was mean.

SOURCE 6 A woman spinning wool, Yorkshire, 1814

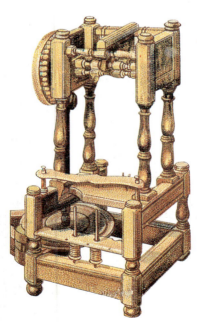

SOURCE 7 Richard Arkwright's water frame spinning machine, 1769

SOURCE 8 Richard Arkwright, sometimes referred to as the 'Father of the factory system'

Arkwright and his partners built their first mill at Nottingham. At the beginning, horses were used to drive the machines. But this was unreliable and expensive. Another, bigger mill was built at Cromford, in Derbyshire, in 1771. This time water power was used. This mill was so successful that other businessmen soon copied it. By 1788, over 40 spinning mills had been built in South Lancashire alone. The 'factory age' had begun.

The mill shown in Source 9 was built in empty countryside, near water. This remoteness had some advantages. For example, it was easier for Arkwright to conceal his new machines from the prying eyes of his competitors. But there were also disadvantages. Make a list of them.

SOURCE 9 Arkwright's mill at Cromford in Derbyshire

SITING A FACTORY

It is important to understand that building a factory was neither easy nor cheap. Machines were expensive, and channels had to be cut, dams built and the waterwheel itself set up. It was vital to site the factory in the right place. A cotton mill needed all these things:

- a good, reliable supply of water
- a good supply of building materials
- a supply of workers
- good transport for getting the raw cotton to the mill and the finished cloth to market
- a good market for the finished cloth.

You need to think about all these problems as you site your own cotton mill.

ACTIVITY

Site your own mill

Imagine that you are a late eighteenth-century businessman. You are going to build a cotton mill somewhere in the Rush Valley. You will also need to build some workers' houses. Look at your map of the area.

a) The contour lines represent the hills overlooking the valley. The closer the lines the steeper the hill.

b) Rushmere, Hilton and Bilbury each have a population of about 500 people. They are quite small farming villages. Most of the farmers and their families do some spinning and weaving in their spare time.

c) Rushmere has a stone quarry.

d) Melton is the nearest town. It has a population of over 10,000 people — really quite large for 1780. Melton has access to a major port.

e) Boats can use the River Rush from the bridge to Melton. West of the bridge (towards the marsh) it becomes shallower and is only navigable by flat-bottomed barges towed by horses. Quarry River will carry the same barges. Be warned! The River Rush has been known to freeze over in winter.

f) In winter the main road linking Rushmere with Melton can only be used by pedestrians and packhorses. In summer it can take horse-drawn waggons. The ruts and potholes make journeys slow.

g) A number of streams or small rivers feed into the River Rush. Only Rapid Falls is fast-flowing and full of water all year round.

1 Study the map of the area and decide where to locate your mill. When you have decided, copy out the map and draw in your mill.

Also mark in your workers' houses and be prepared to explain why you have put them there.

2 Next, copy out the 'Factors of Production' grid. This shows all the things which your mill will need if it is going to be a success. In the empty columns explain how your mill will be supplied with each of these factors of production.

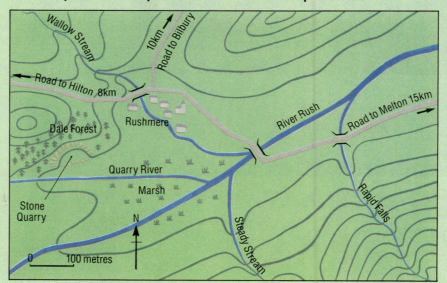

The Rush Valley

Factors of Production		
Building materials		
Water power		
Raw cotton		
Workers		
Market for finished cloth		
Transport		

Factory buildings

The North of England still has many old mills and factories. Some are now ruins, but others, like Samuel Gregg's mill at Styal, have been turned into museums. Historians can learn quite a lot about early factories and their owners from examining these mills.

SOURCE 10 Mill at Summer Seat

SOURCE 11 Saltaire Mill, Bradford

1 These mills seem to be built to a similar pattern. Describe their main features.

2 Remember that the original source of power for the mills was water. What evidence is there that a new source of power was developed later?

3 Why do these mill buildings have so many windows?

4 What can these mill buildings *not* tell us about life and work in the early factories?

5 How do these early mills differ from modern factory buildings?

6 Do you think it is important that buildings like these should be preserved? Discuss your views with the rest of the class.

Siting and building the factory was not the end of the story. Factory owners next had to decide on the number of machines to install, the number and type of workers to employ, the hours of work, the rates of pay and so forth.

Building a new factory was a big risk. The risk was only worth taking if the factory owners could make a big profit. They had no previous experience to draw on. Inevitably they got some things wrong, and it was often their workers who suffered.

ACTIVITY

Organise your mill

> Rushmere,
> Lancashire
> 6 May 1780
>
> Dear Mr Heywood, I humbly request your help on the following questions to enable the work on your new mill to proceed smoothly and speedily. I would be grateful for full and detailed explanations of your decisions.
>
> 1. The builders need to know how many windows to put in on each of the mill's three floors. Many large windows will admit plenty of light but will also distract the workers.
>
> 2. Do you favour employing men, women or children? The new machines do not demand much strength to operate. The more machines you can crowd into your mill, the more yarn you will produce and the greater the profit.
>
> 3. How many days a week and how many hours a day should your labourers work? What breaks for lunch, tea, etc. would you recommend? Remember that workers might spend their free time in the ale house plotting against you.
>
> 4. What rates of pay would you suggest? If wages are too generous, it might make it difficult to get whole families into the mill. (The head of the household would be able to support the whole family by his efforts alone.) Also it might be difficult to get them to work enough hours. Remember, men cost more than women to employ, and women cost more than children. Finally, might I suggest you pay wages in tokens rather than money. The workers can exchange these for food, etc. in your factory shop.
>
> 5. Please provide a list of rules to control the behaviour of your workers. What punishments would you recommend? Remember that there is a growing population and much unemployment. You can afford to be strict.
>
> I remain your loyal & obedient servant,
>
> Nathaniel Shed
> Manager

This activity is designed to increase your understanding of the difficulties facing the first factory owners. Could you have overcome them?

You have just received a letter from your manager, Nathaniel Shed. You have put him in charge of the final stages of building your mill and employing workers. He needs your decision on a number of matters, as outlined in his letter.

Before replying to each of the points in his letter, join up with a partner and look at Sources 12 to 22. Discuss and answer the questions on them. The Sources should give you some clues as to how mill owners tried to overcome the early problems. [Remember – the letter has been made up but all the Sources are real.]

After working through the Sources, *each* write a letter to Nathaniel Shed, giving your answers to his questions. Explain your decisions in as much detail as possible. You could then display all your letters.

The employment of women and children

In 1833 two-thirds of the workers in the textile mills were women and children. The managers and overlookers (supervisors) were men.

1 Why did mill owners employ mainly women to operate the machines, but men to be supervisors?

2 Notice the young boy crawling under the machine on the right in Source 13. What do you suppose he is doing?

3 Why did mill owners find child labourers so useful?

4 How do both of these pictures (Sources 12 and 13) suggest that it could be dangerous working in these early factories?

5 Do these two Sources give a similar or a different impression of life in mid-nineteenth century mills?

SOURCE 12 Mill girls operating power looms, 1835

SOURCE 13 Spinning machines operating in a cloth mill, about 1850

SOURCE 14 The disciplining of child workers, 1840

Employing children was often justified by saying they were quite happy in their work. But there were critics of child labour. Source 14 is a contemporary cartoon, published to show how badly children were treated in factories.

> 1 **How did factory managers make sure children worked hard?**
>
> 2 **It is obvious that the cartoonist was against the employment of children in mills. Does the bias of the cartoon make it useless as a piece of historical evidence? Why?**

James M'Nish, reporting to a Parliamentary Committee in 1831, explained why employers preferred very young, small children (Source 15). Some mill owners wrote to the Poor Law Authorities, offering to employ pauper children. The Poor Law Authorities were responsible for caring for pauper children in their parish. Pauper children were those without homes, money and sometimes even parents. The Poor Law Authorities were pleased to hand the children over to factory owners to house, feed and clothe. The children worked — unpaid — in the mills, in virtual slavery (see Sources 16 and 17).

SOURCE 17 Pauper apprentices, early nineteenth century

Has this employer kept his promise to clothe and feed the pauper children in his mill?

Working hours

Working hours in the mills were usually very long. Source 18 is an extract from a Parliamentary Enquiry into Factories in 1832. It shows that a working day of more than eighteen hours was not unknown — and that was for children.

> **SOURCE 18**
>
> *Question:* At what time in the morning in the busy season did those girls go to the mill?
>
> *Answer:* In the busy time, for about six weeks, they have gone at about 3 o'clock in the morning, and ended at ten or nearly half-past ten at night.
>
> *Question:* What intervals were allowed for rest or refreshment during these nineteen hours of labour?
>
> *Answer:* Breakfast a quarter of an hour, and dinner half an hour, and drinking a quarter of an hour.
>
> *Evidence of Samuel Coulson, a tailor at Stanningley near Leeds, with three daughters in the mills.*

Long working hours were bad for the workers themselves. How might they have been bad for factory owners too? Think whether it is really possible to work hard and well for eighteen hours a day.

Wage rates

Factory owners kept wages low in order to make more money themselves and to encourage workers to turn up. If workers were poorly paid they would have to come into work every day. In 1790, at Samuel Gregg's mill at Styal in Cheshire, wages ranged from 1s. 6d. (7½p) a week for a doffer — the child whose job it was to change the spindles — to 15s. (75p) a week for an overlooker. At Arkwright's Cromford Mill in 1786 the average adult weekly wage was just 3s. 6d. (17½p).

Working conditions

There were no regulations covering working conditions in factory rooms. A Factory Report of 1833 commented on the conditions (Source 19).

> **SOURCE 19**
>
> The old and small mills [are] dirty, low-roofed, ill-ventilated; no conveniences for washing or dressing; machinery not boxed in; some of the flats [rooms] so low that it is scarcely possible to stand upright.

1 Why do you suppose the mill owners paid so little attention to working conditions?

2 Why didn't they have lavatories, canteens, etc. in their mills?

3 Compare Source 20 with Source 17 — how do they differ?

SOURCE 20 The winding room of an early nineteenth-century cotton mill

Accidents

As machinery was not boxed in, working in the mills could be dangerous. Robert Blincoe described one accident (Source 21).

SOURCE 21

The forefinger of his left hand was caught, and almost before he could cry out, off was the first joint . . . he clapped the mangled joint, streaming with blood to the finger, and ran off to the surgeon, who very composedly [calmly] put the parts together again and sent him back to the mill.

Robert Blincoe had been an apprentice in a mill at Litton in Derbyshire, in the early 1800s. He described the accident (Source 21) several years later, when he was grown up. Explain how reliable you think this Source is.

The accident that Blincoe witnessed was certainly not an isolated episode. John Moss, who visited several different cotton mills, claimed that accidents to children were frequent and occasionally even fatal: 'Very often their [children's] fingers were crushed, and one had his arm broken' (John Moss, 1810).

But the factory owners refused to take action. They blamed the frequency of accidents on the carelessness and clumsiness of the children. Their only solution was to employ more 'strappers' to make sure the children stayed awake.

Disciplining the workforce

Before the Industrial Revolution workers used to have busy and slack times of year. Harvesting and haymaking were the most hectic period. By contrast, factory work was not affected by the weather or the season of the year. The new factory owners had to make their workforce work regular hours all year round. They had to get them to carry out the same, often boring, tasks over and over again. They had many ways of doing this.

Some owners made workers 'clock in' and always sacked them if they were late. Many drew up strict rules. If these were broken, there were fines (see Source 22). Children were sometimes beaten.

SOURCE 22

Fines   s. d.

Any spinner found with his window open 1 0

Any spinner found dirty at his work 1 0

Any spinner found washing himself 1 0

Any spinner heard whistling 1 0

Any spinner being five minutes after last bell rings 1 0

Any spinner having a little waste on his spindles 1 0

Any spinner being sick and cannot find another spinner to give satisfaction must pay for steam for the day 6 0

Any spinner going further than the roving room when fetching 1 0

From a list of fines published in a strike pamphlet by spinners of Tyldesley, 1823

---

1 Compare the fines (Source 22) with the wage rates. How large were these fines?

2 Do you think these rules kept the workers in order?

Urbanisation

After 1785, machines started to be powered by steam, not water. This meant that factories no longer had to be near fast-flowing streams. They moved from the countryside to towns and cities to be near the main roads and the canals which carried the coal needed to produce the steam. In towns they were also near the skilled engineers who could repair the new steam engines.

Towns grew fast (see Source 23). Manchester had fewer than 10,000 inhabitants in 1700 but grew to 75,000 by 1801. By 1851 more than half the people of England and Wales lived in towns which had over 50,000 people.

The towns grew so fast that living conditions were terrible. Source 24 describes a district of Newcastle in 1842.

SOURCE 24

On the north-east side of the town is a stagnant gutter. The blood from several killing shops runs into it. The great cause of dirt and dirty habits in northern towns is the state of the privies [toilets] used in common by the people who live in small houses and single rooms. No one wants the job of keeping them clean, and some individuals really have pleasure in dirtying them; and when the place gets filthy, they use the outside, or even the footpaths of the streets.

The overcrowded, dirty living conditions bred diseases. The worst of these was cholera, which was spread through dirty drinking water. Between 1846 and 1849 50,000 people died from cholera in Britain. This epidemic finally persuaded the government to take some action to make towns cleaner places.

1 List all the different types of pollution that you can see in Source 25.

2 Get together with a partner. One partner should list all the advantages of living in towns or cities today while the other can list the disadvantages. See who can compile the longer list. Then, as a whole class, discuss your lists and decide whether you think living in towns and cities is a good idea or not.

3 Look at Source 23. Which town gained most people between 1831 and 1931?

4 Which towns lost people after 1931? Why do you think this might have been?

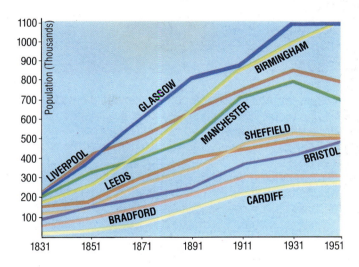

SOURCE 23 The growth of towns, 1831–1951

SOURCE 25 A London street in the 1850s

Wealth and poverty

The Industrial Revolution increased the gap between rich and poor. Some people, like the new class of factory owners, made large fortunes. In time, some of the skilled workers and mill hands also became better off.

SOURCE 26 Women workers at Dean Mills, 1851

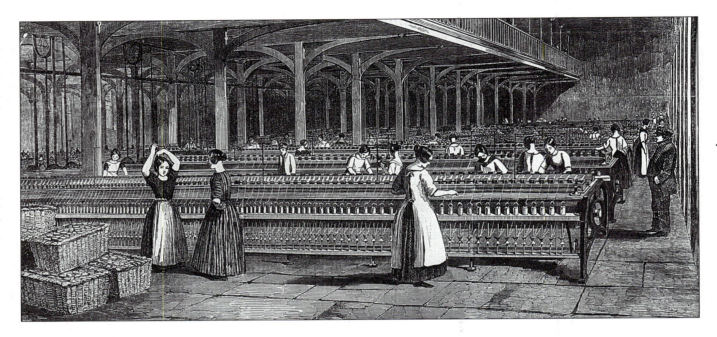

Source 26 shows mill girls in the mid-nineteenth century. Notice how well dressed they are. They could only buy these clothes because factories were starting to produce goods in such large quantities and so cheaply that a large number of people could now afford them.

In 1887, in his *Essays on Finance*, Robert Giffen spoke of the improved lifestyle of the workers (Source 27).

However, not all of 'the masses' were doing so well. While the wages of some workers were rising, other workers lost their jobs altogether. Newly invented machines took jobs from skilled workers like the handloom weavers who had previously earned very good wages. They were reduced to unemployment and poverty.

The handloom weavers and other redundant workers often showed their frustration and anger by smashing up the new machinery (see Source 28).

Those who could not find other work often ended up in the workhouse, where they were treated as little better than criminals (see Source 29).

SOURCE 27

The working classes of the United Kingdom have enjoyed a great improvement in wages in the last fifty years, an improvement roughly estimated at 50 to 100 per cent; the hours of work have been shortened in the same period 20 per cent; the condition of the masses has in fact improved vastly, as is shown by . . . the increased consumption per head of tea, sugar and the like articles, by the extension of popular education, the reduction of crime and poverty, and the increase of savings bank deposits.

SOURCE 28

We the framework knitters declare to all hosiers, lace manufacturers and proprietors of frames that we will break and destroy all manner of frames whatsoever . . . and all frames that do not pay the regular prices heretofore agreed.
Given under my hand this first day of January, 1812, at Ned Lud's office, Sherwood Forest.

Of course, there had always been poverty. But in the middle of so much wealth this poverty now seemed worse.

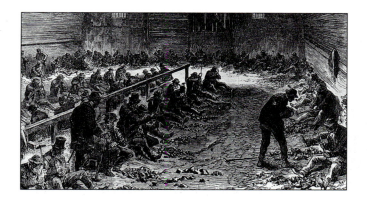

SOURCE 29 The 'labour yard' at Bethnal Green, East London, 1868. Food was exchanged for hard labour.

1 Look at Source 27. **List the ways in which the lives of the workers had been improved.**

2 Look at Source 29. **What 'work' do these unemployed men appear to be doing?**

3 Can you think of any skilled workers today whose jobs are threatened by the invention of new machines? Make a list of the jobs.

Trade unions

Some men and women decided to combine together so that they could persuade employers to improve wages and working conditions. This was the beginning of the trade union movement.

Employers were suspicious of trade unions and did all they could to suppress them. Parliament passed the Combination Acts (1799 and 1800) which forbade workers to combine 'in restraint of trade'. To survive, the unions had to operate as secret societies. This lasted until 1824 when the Combination Acts were repealed. In 1825 an Act of Parliament said it was no longer a crime for workmen and women to belong to a trade union as long as they did not 'molest or intimidate' anyone. Almost any trade union activity could be seen as 'molesting or intimidating' and so employers continued to bring trade union members before the law courts.

The most notorious case was in 1834 when six farm labourers from Tolpuddle in Dorset were convicted for taking an illegal oath on joining a trade union (see Source 31). They were sentenced to seven years' deportation to the dreaded Penal Colony of Botany Bay in Australia. The harshness of the sentence caused a national outcry.

Look at Source 30.
1 What was the job of the women who joined this trade union?

2 The motto of this early trade union was 'United to Protect'.
  a Why was it necessary for the workers to unite before they could hope to improve their working conditions?
  b What sort of things did the workers want to protect?

3 Try to think of some other suitable mottos for the early trade unions.

SOURCE 30 An early trade union membership card

SOURCE 31 The Tolpuddle Martyrs (a 19th-century print)

By the 1850s trade unions of skilled workers were firmly established. They organised accident insurance, sick pay, burial clubs and other benefits for their members. It was not until the 1871 Trades Dispute Act that strikes were recognised as legal and not until 1875 that the government allowed strikers to peacefully 'picket' – that is, to persuade other men and women not to go into work during a strike.

This was by no means the end of the story. But by the 1870s it was clear that trade unions were here to stay. Slowly but surely, by organising strikes to get higher wages and by organising help such as benefit schemes, the trade unions improved the lives of the workers.

Factory reform

When the Industrial Revolution began, the government left the factory owners free to deal with wages, prices, working conditions and hours of work. As we have seen, this could lead to very bad conditions for the workers. Of course, some of the new employers – men like Robert Owen and Sir Robert Peel – were caring men. At his New Lanark Mill in Scotland, Owen built rows of good quality houses (see Source 32) and provided a school and a community hall for his workers. He reduced the hours of work at his factory, put up the wages and refused to employ very young children.

But very few factory owners were this caring. In the end, REFORMERS like Lord Shaftesbury and Richard Oastler collected such damning evidence about conditions in factories that Parliament had to take action. During the 19th century a series of Factory Acts was passed:

FACTORY ACT	DETAILS
1819 Factory Act	Prohibited the employment of children under 9 years of age. It remained largely unenforced because of the lack of Factory Inspectors.
1833 Factory Act	Paid inspectors were appointed to visit factories and enforce the law. No children under 9 to be employed. Children aged 9 to 12 not to work more than an 8-hour day and to have two hours daily schooling. 'Young people' aged 13 to 18 not to work more than 69 hours a week.
1844 Factory Act	Women were to be treated n the same way as 'young people'. Dangerous machinery had to be fenced off.
1847 Factory Act	Maximum 10-hour day fixed for women and children 13–18 years old.
1867 Factory and Workshop Act	The above rules and regulations extended to all factory workers, not just those in textile mills.
1897 Workmen's Compensation Act	If workers were ill or injured as a result of their job they were to receive at least half-pay until they were well.

These Factory Acts were important not only because they improved working conditions. They also got the government used to the idea of playing a part in the lives of ordinary people. In later years, governments passed other laws providing free education, old age pensions, free health care, unemployment payments, and a range of other benefits.

SOURCE 32 Robert Owen's model mill at New Lanark, Scotland

1 Why did the early factory reforms apply to women and children only?

2 The 1833 Factory Act fixed a maximum 69-hour working week for 'young people'. What is the average working week in Britain today?

3 Make a list of all the benefits the state provides for people today.

Industrialisation today

Britain began to industrialise just over 200 years ago. The Industrial Revolution was not a sudden, rapid event, as most political revolutions are (see Unit 2). The changes took place gradually, over a long period of time.

New machines were invented. People discovered new ways of powering them. The goods which were produced were moved around the country by new means of transport.

An 'industrial revolution' is still taking place today. The manufacture of the silicon chip has led to all sorts of advances in computer technology. Nuclear power is becoming more and more important.

Britain was one of the first countries to industrialise. Other countries followed and have now overtaken Britain in industrial strength – the United States and Japan, for example. Developing countries are trying hard to industrialise to gain wealth and power.

As we have seen, industrialisation has had a huge impact on the way people in Britain live. There is still debate about whether the changes have definitely been for the better.

ASSESSMENT

Change

1 a List all the important ways in which the Industrial Revolution changed working people's lives.
   b Which of these changes do you think was the most important of all?
   c Now divide your list into two – 'Changes for the better' and 'Changes for the worse'. Which list is the longer?

Continuity

2 The Industrial Revolution introduced changes which continue to decide the way we live today. Consider your own lifestyle – your house, your hobbies, your clothes, your entertainments, your holidays, your food, and so forth. Make a list of all the things you would not be able to enjoy if there had not been an Industrial Revolution. Can you think of some results of the Industrial Revolution which you could happily do without?

Continuity

3 The Industrial Revolution was not a sudden or brief event. It lasted many years. Indeed, there have been other 'industrial revolutions' in Britain since the first one. You can probably think of inventions in your own lifetime which have totally changed the way people live and work. Produce a chart with a description of these inventions on one side and an explanation of their importance on the other. Do you think that any recent invention has been as important in its consequences as Arkwright's invention of the water frame?

Inference

4 Examine the details of the Factory Acts passed between 1819 and 1897. What do you infer from these about the reasons for the slow pace at which government regulation of factories was introduced? Make a list of all the possible reasons for the slowness of the progress made.

Bias and reliability

5 Most of the written evidence in this chapter comes from middle-class people. Workers only tended to record their views on factory life when questioned by Parliamentary Commissions. Why was this? Do you think this affects the picture of factory life we get? How?

Cross-reference

6 Look forward to Unit 2 on the French Revolution. In what ways was this revolution similar to the Industrial Revolution? In what ways was it different? Explain why both events deserve to be called 'revolutions'.

2

THE FRENCH REVOLUTION

The execution of a king

ON 21ST JANUARY 1793, Louis Capet, formerly King Louis XVI of France, was driven in his carriage to the scaffold in the Place de la Revolution in Paris. Abbé Edgworth, an Irish priest who accompanied him, described the scene (Source 1).

SOURCE 2 Louis Capet's head is shown to the crowd.

SOURCE 1

The coach arrived amid a great silence. . . . The space around the scaffold was edged with cannon and as far as the eye could see was an armed crowd. . . . As soon as the King had got out of the coach, three of the executioners surrounded him and tried to remove his top clothes. He pushed them away with dignity and took off his coat himself, his collar and his shirt, and made himself ready with his own hands.

A Deputy to the CONVENTION, Mercier, who was in the crowd of spectators, described what followed (Source 3).

SOURCE 3

His blood flows; cries of joy from 80,000 armed men rend the air. His blood flows and there are people who dip a fingertip, a quill, a scrap of paper in it. One tastes it: 'It is vilely salt!' An executioner at the scaffold side sells small bundles of his hair; people buy the ribbon that tied it. Everyone carries off a small bundle of his clothing or some other blood-stained remnant. The whole populace go by, arm in arm, laughing, talking as if returning from some festivity. . . . The taverns on the bloody square had their wine bottles emptied as usual. They sold cakes and patties around the beheaded body, which was put in the wicker basket of the common criminal.

The rest of Europe was horrified by King Louis' execution. Many people still believed that kings ruled by 'Divine Right' — that they were God's agents on earth. To murder a king was an unspeakable crime. If a king could be executed then no one was safe. The rulers and noblemen of the rest of Europe shuddered to think of the disorder and chaos that might follow. How could France, the most civilised country in Europe, have fallen so low?

1 In what ways do the Sources suggest that some French people still believed in the 'Divine' or supernatural powers of kingship?

2 Do you think the authors of Sources 1 and 3 supported or opposed the king? Explain your answer.

3 Look at the picture of the execution (Source 2). In what way does this picture agree with or conflict with the eye-witness accounts?

People were right to be alarmed by the execution of Louis XVI. Within a year revolutionary France was at war with most of Europe, including Britain. The wars dragged on for over twenty years and released ideas and passions that were to change the world (see Source 4).

SOURCE 4

The French Revolution ushered in the modern world, for the problems that it posed have been the mainspring of all subsequent political revolutions.

R. B. Jones, *The French Revolution*, 1967

AIMS

This unit is mainly concerned with causes — why things happen. It is easy to slip into the mistake of thinking that all historical events are inevitable, that they had to happen and could only have happened in one particular way. It is equally tempting to assume that events are brought about by one big cause. This unit will show that this is not the case.

When we look at the causes of the French Revolution we shall see that no large group of people in France wanted a REVOLUTION in 1789. It came about almost accidentally as a result of many different groups of people doing what they thought would be best for themselves.

This unit will also show how difficult it is to control and direct events. The French Revolution was to take directions which no one could have predicted and very few people intended. The consequences of events can be as complex as their causes. In the case of the French Revolution the consequences were felt far away from France for many years after the Revolution itself.

In the previous unit we looked at one particular type of revolution, an industrial revolution. We saw that this type of revolution can change society, but it is usually gradual. A political revolution, on the other hand, is often sudden and violent. The word 'revolution' means the complete turning upside down of society — so that one system is replaced by another system which is often completely different. A revolution can involve every aspect of government, the economy and society, and is usually based on a particular idea or belief.

23

THE CAUSES OF THE FRENCH REVOLUTION

The rich and the poor

Most revolutions spring from divisions in society. In 18th-century France there was a small group of 'haves' and a large mass of 'have-nots'. Most of the wealth, top jobs and privileges were enjoyed by just half a million noblemen and high-ranking churchmen. By contrast, the remaining 22 million peasants, workers and merchants did most of the hard work and paid most of the taxes. Though they paid for the government, they were not allowed to have any say in how it managed the affairs of the country.

ACTIVITY

Peasants and noblemen

Examine Sources 5–10. They contrast the life of the poor and the life of the wealthy in late eighteenth-century France. Make two lists. In one, list the main features of a peasant's life, and in the other the main features of a nobleman's life. Then summarise the most important difference between the two lifestyles.

The life of the peasantry

Most of the French people at this time were peasants, trying to scratch a living from the land. An Englishman, Arthur Young, described his meeting with a peasant woman in Lorraine in July 1789 (Source 5).

SOURCE 5

Walking up a long hill to rest my horse, I was joined by a poor woman, who complained of the times, and that it was a sad country. On my demanding her reasons, she said her husband had only a small piece of land, one cow and a poor little house, yet he had 20 kg of wheat and three chickens to pay as quit rent to one lord, and 75 kg of oats, one chicken and one sow to pay to another, besides very heavy tailles [land tax] and other taxes. She had seven children...
This woman, at no great distance, might have been taken for sixty or seventy, her figure was so bent and her face as furrowed and hardened by labour; but she said she was only twenty-eight.

Source 6 is a contemporary French cartoon showing a peasant being crushed by the *taille, impots* (taxes) and the *corvée* (forced labour). Peasants also had to pay taxes (called tithes) to the Catholic Church. The cartoon is no exaggeration; it was not unusual for peasants to pay as much as 75% of their income in taxes.

SOURCE 6 A French cartoon of 1789

1 Look at Source 6. Who are the two figures standing on the stone meant to represent?

2 What can this cartoon tell us about the life of peasants in eighteenth-century France?

3 This cartoon is taking the peasants' side, although it is unlikely that a peasant actually drew it. Who might have sympathised with the peasants enough to speak up for them in this way?

4 Compare Sources 5 and 6.
  a In what way do these two Sources agree?
  b Which one of these Sources do you think would have been more likely to stir up the anger of the French peasants? Explain why.

The four contemporary prints in Source 7 reveal some of the other burdens and humiliations the peasants had to suffer.

SOURCE 7

◄ Every time a peasant woman took produce to market she had to pay a customs duty or tax at a toll booth. This print suggests that husbands and fathers may have disliked these toll keepers for another reason as well. What was it?

Peasants were often forced by recruiting officers to enlist in the army. Who do you think would farm the peasants' land while they were away? ►

◄ This peasant is in trouble with a gamekeeper. All wild game belonged to the nobes. It was a serious offence to be caught poaching. The offender was often sentenced to the galleys (prison ships). Why, knowing this, did peasants continue to poach?

Peasants feared and hated magistrates — they charged high fees and often seemed to be on the side of the rich and powerful. Is there any evidence in this picture that magistrates were themselves quite wealthy? ►

Why, do you suppose, this section contains no written sources by the peasants themselves?

The life of the aristocracy

Pierre Goubert, a historian, has described the privileges of French noblemen in the eighteenth century (Source 9).

SOURCE 9

There was clearly a typical noble lifestyle – lavish entertaining, horsemanship, being a good shot, fighting no duels with commoners and, above all, never working with one's hands at profitable, base and mechanical jobs. . . . In most regiments an ordinary lieutenancy could not usually be granted to anyone who was not able to prove four degrees of nobility. . . . It was usual for the King to award the important and even minor [government] posts to his faithful noblemen. . . . Since the Concordat of 1516 the King kept the right of choosing almost all bishops and most abbots. He almost always gave these posts to noblemen. . . . Because in principle they helped the King by serving in his army, the nobility were exempt from paying taxes.

Pierre Goubert, L'Ancien Régime, 1969

1 **What do you suppose Goubert means by 'profitable, base and mechanical jobs'?**

2 **Which of the privileges listed in Source 9 would have been most important to a nobleman? Explain your answer.**

3 **Look at Source 8. What can we learn from this painting about the lifestyle of the aristocracy?**

4 **Source 8 was painted at the time of the French Revolution. Source 9 was written nearly two hundred years later. Does that make the picture a more reliable source of evidence for someone wishing to find out about aristocratic life in eighteenth-century France? Explain your answer.**

You may think that we need look no further for the causes of the French Revolution. Certainly British people at the time thought that the contrast between the wealth of the aristocrats and the poverty of the peasants had much to do with the troubles in France. Some British people could not resist comparing the poor French peasants with the better-off British labouring classes. When Arthur Young visited France in the 1780s he reported that the French workers 'are 75% less at their ease, worse fed, clothed and worse supported than the same class in England'.

But the existence of a large mass of poor downtrodden peasants was not, by itself, enough to cause a revolution. If that had been the case then one might have expected a revolution in Russia where the peasants were even poorer and worse treated than in France. In fact, peasants usually lacked the education and organisation to make a revolution by themselves, whatever their complaints against their masters. The peasants could provide the anger and the resentment but other people had to provide the leadership.

So there must have been other causes of the French Revolution in 1789. What were they?

The king

King Louis XVI of France claimed that he had 'absolute power'. He summed up the meaning of this when he said 'The state is myself', and 'The thing is law because I wish it'. As he was later to discover, he was not quite as all-powerful as he thought. None the less, he was very important to the government of France. The massive power which the king held meant that the strength of the government depended largely on his personality. Unfortunately, Louis XVI lacked the ruthlessness, energy and decisiveness needed for the job.

The Abbot of Veri, who knew the king, described his character (Source 10).

SOURCE 10

One can see the king spending his afternoons in his office watching people arriving at Versailles through his telescope. He often occupies himself sweeping up or knocking in nails. . . . He has a sturdy enough intelligence, simple tastes, an honest heart and a true soul. But on the other hand he has a tendency for indecisiveness, a feeble will.

The king's 'feeble will' was clear in his dealings with his wife, Marie Antoinette. She was an Austrian princess with an iron will, extravagant tastes and little love for the French people who were now her subjects. Comte de Mirabeau, a nobleman who later supported the Revolution, complained about her influence (Source 11).

SOURCE 11

The king has only one man about him, his wife.

Source 12 is a royal portrait by Callet. It shows Louis XVI to have been a large man who clearly enjoyed the good things in life. One of his courtiers, called Bachaumont, reported on the king's eating habits (Source 13).

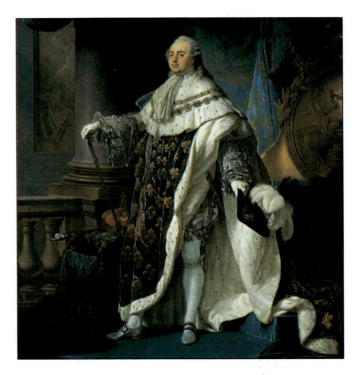

SOURCE 12 Louis XVI, by Antoine Callet

SOURCE 13

The king eats four cutlets, a fried chicken, six eggs in gravy and a slice of ham and drinks a bottle and a half of champagne; he gets dressed, leaves for the hunt, and returns to dine with an incredible appetite.

And this meal was only his breakfast!

1 Use Sources 10, 11, 12 and 13 to write down five statements about Louis XVI.

2 Louis XVI was strongly influenced by his wife. Why, do you think, this made him unpopular with his subjects?

3 Do you think Louis XVI was a bad man? Explain your answer.

Louis was certainly not a great king. His own gluttony and his wife's extravagance did not make him popular with the mass of his peasant subjects. More importantly, his indecision and dithering nature meant that he was not the man to deal with a crisis. Quite simply, Louis lacked the qualities needed for leadership and for firm, fair government.

27

The influence of new ideas

Eighteenth-century France produced a large number of writers and philosophers who looked carefully at the world around them and criticised it. Their ideas gradually spread. They encouraged people to think again about the laws, customs and attitudes which they had always accepted as natural. In particular they questioned the Church's claim that God had made everyone with a fixed role in life and that it was therefore pointless trying to change things. The philosophers argued that any person could improve their life, and the lives of others, by taking action (see Sources 14–16).

> **SOURCE 14**
>
> *Man is born free, but everywhere he is in chains.*
>
> J. J. Rousseau, The Social Contract, 1762
>
> *. . . in the natural order, men are all equal.*
>
> J. J. Rousseau, Emile, 1762

> **SOURCE 15**
>
> There is no true sovereign, there can be no true lawmaker, but the people.
>
> D. Diderot, 1713–84

> **SOURCE 16**
>
> *The thing to complain of is not the badness of men, but the ignorance of lawmakers.*
>
> Helvétius, On the Mind, 1758

---

1 a **In what ways were these new ideas a threat to the power of King Louis XVI?**
  b **Which class of people in France probably remained ignorant of this new thinking?**

2 **Why were these ideas considered to be 'revolutionary' at the time? Would they be considered revolutionary today?**

These writers' most important achievement was to make people more critical of the way they were governed. The philosophers did not produce any clear programme for particular reforms but their new ideas added to the demand for change in France in the 1780s.

The American War of Independence

In 1776 the 13 British colonies in North America revolted. They issued their Declaration of Independence, and by 1783 had won their freedom from Britain, to become the United States of America. France helped the Americans against Britain. Her motive was revenge. France had earlier been defeated by Britain during the Seven Years War (1756–63).

SOURCE 17 Marquis de Lafayette, a general who became one of the leaders of the Revolution.

Many of the French soldiers fighting in America were influenced by the new ideas about liberty and the 'Rights of Man' (see Source 17). Having fought to win freedom for another country they were less ready to put up with tyranny in their own country. They supported Thomas Jefferson's claim in the Declaration of Independence that it was the right of all citizens to choose their own government and to resist and change a bad government (see Source 18).

> **SOURCE 18**
>
> **It is the right of the people to alter or abolish it [a bad government] and to institute new government, laying its foundations on such principles and organising its power in such form as to them shall seem most likely to effect their safety and happiness.**
>
> **Declaration of Independence, 1776**

But French involvement in the American War of Independence had an even more important result. The war was enormously expensive and helped to bring about the bankruptcy of the French government.

The following BUDGET Report of March 1788 shows just how serious the situation was:

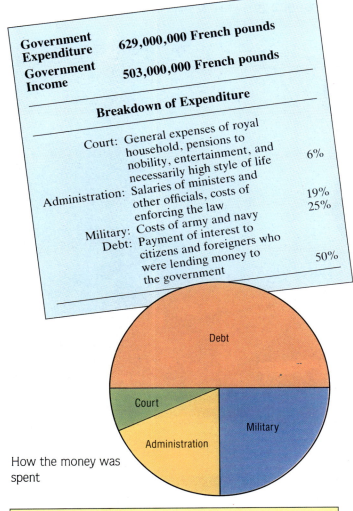

| Government Expenditure | 629,000,000 French pounds |
| Government Income | 503,000,000 French pounds |

Breakdown of Expenditure

Court:	General expenses of royal household, pensions to nobility, entertainment, and necessarily high style of life	6%
Administration:	Salaries of ministers and other officials, costs of enforcing the law	19%
Military:	Costs of army and navy	25%
Debt:	Payment of interest to citizens and foreigners who were lending money to the government	50%

How the money was spent

1 Look carefully at the Budget Report of 1788. Which one of these items do you think most angered the French people and why?

2 Divide into groups of three or four. Each group must discuss ways of solving this economic crisis. Make a list of possible solutions and pass it on to the king (teacher) for consideration. Remember that you are looking for ways of raising extra cash.

It was this financial crisis that triggered off the Revolution. It may not have been the most important cause but it was certainly the most *immediate* cause.

The meeting of the Estates General

The king's solution to his money problems was to impose new taxes on the nobility. You can imagine their reaction. They were furious and refused to pay. In the end their opposition forced the king to call a meeting in 1789 of the Estates General – an assembly of all the classes or 'estates' of France. The nobility hoped to use this meeting to defeat the king's tax proposals and to actually increase their own powers and privileges. But other people had very different ideas:

1 The peasants in the countryside and the workers in the towns hoped to use the meeting to free themselves from some of the taxes and to improve their standard of living. In 1788 the corn harvest had totally failed and so the poor were suffering even more than usual. Source 19 shows how the price of bread soared. Hunger and despair had already produced riots and disturbances throughout France by the time the Estates General met.

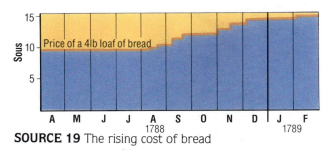

Price of a 4lb loaf of bread

SOURCE 19 The rising cost of bread

2 The middle class – magistrates, lawyers, teachers, bankers – also had plans of their own. These people were usually educated, talented and wealthy and yet they played no part in the government of France. They had no intention of letting the nobility strengthen their hold on the best jobs. Thus they decided to use the disorder in the countryside to gain a share in privilege and power for themselves. When the Estates General met in May 1789 the middle class demanded a change in its organisation. When this was refused they broke away to form the National Assembly.

They did not aim to create a democratic government where all men had a say in running the country. They simply believed that the middle-class men of property had a right to join with the nobility in governing France. They soon discovered that it was very difficult to demand rights and liberties for one class without encouraging other classes to make similar demands. The middle class started a revolution which would go much further than they had ever intended.

Look at Source 20 which is a contemporary cartoon of the events of 1789.

1 Which sections of French society are represented by the two figures on the left? Why are they frightened?

2 Which classes of society made up the Third Estate?

3 What evidence is there that the person who drew this cartoon expected the Third Estate to resort to violence?

SOURCE 20 'Reveil du Tiers Etat' — The Awakening of the Third Estate

ASSESSMENT

Cause and consequence

1 Historians usually divide the causes of events into long-term (those that had been there for a long time), and immediate (those which immediately preceded the event and triggered it off). Divide the causes of the French Revolution into long-term and immediate.

Cause and consequence

2 Select one cause which you believe to have been more important than the others. Explain your choice.

Role of the individual

3 The king's character has been suggested as one of the causes of the French Revolution. Do you think that individuals, however powerful, can change the course of history? Explain your answer. You could refer back to Alfred the Great (Book 1) and to King Charles I (Book 2) as other examples of individuals who had an important impact on events.

FROM LIBERTY TO TERROR

The middle-class men who started the Revolution were idealists. They believed it was possible to create a perfect society. On 26th August 1789, they issued a Declaration of the Rights of Man (Source 21).

SOURCE 21

Men are born and remain free and equal in rights. . . . These rights are liberty, property, security and resistance to oppression. . . . Every man is innocent until proved guilty. . . . Every citizen may speak, write and print freely. . . . No one may be disturbed for his opinions even in religion.

Just five years later, on 10 June 1794, virtually the same men passed a very different law (Source 22).

SOURCE 22

The Revolutionary Tribunal is set up to punish the enemies of the people. The enemies of the people are those who seek to destroy public liberty either by force or by cunning. . . . Those who have tried to hinder the provisioning of Paris or create scarcity in the Republic. . . . Those who have tried to spread defeatism . . . who have spread false news. . . . The penalty for all offences under the control of the Revolutionary Tribunal is death. . . . Every citizen has the right to seize conspirators. . . . The law does not grant . . . [defence counsel] . . . to conspirators.

1 Discuss Source 21 in pairs.
   a Do you agree with all of these Rights of Man? (You should think of Man as a term used to cover all people of both sexes.) Do you want to add any others? Make a list of the basic human rights you think everyone is entitled to today. Compare your list with others in the class.
   b 'Liberty' can be a dangerous idea. What problems might there be in granting everyone unlimited freedom?

2 Still in pairs, examine Source 22. In what ways does this law differ from the Declaration of the Rights of Man?

3 Share your answers to all these questions in a class discussion.

Clearly something had gone badly wrong with the Revolution. The high hopes for liberty and equality of 1789 had given way to a ruthless DICTATORSHIP by 1794. What had taken place in the intervening five years?

In 1791 a constitution passed by the National Assembly transferred most real power to the new Legislative Assembly. The king lost his control over lawmaking, the army and justice. In 1792, under directions from the Legislative Assembly, Louis declared war on Austria and Prussia. Many of the revolutionaries favoured a war because they believed this would rally the French people behind their new government. Louis had his own reasons for wanting war. He hoped his fellow European monarchs would be able to defeat France and restore his full powers.

In its early stages the war went very badly for France. Many Frenchmen blamed their defeats on the king – after all, he was married to an Austrian! Mounting suspicion of the king led to his deposition. On 22 September 1792, the Convention, which had replaced the Legislative Assembly, proclaimed that France was now a republic – there would be no more kings and noblemen.

But this was not the end of France's problems. By mid-1793 France was at war with most of Europe (see Source 23). The British, Dutch and Austrian armies were invading from the north, the Prussians from the north-east, the Piedmontese and Austrians from the east, and the Spaniards from the south. In addition, the British navy was attacking France's Atlantic and Mediterranean coasts.

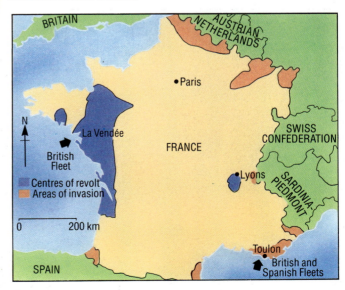

SOURCE 23 The Revolution under attack

Within France itself there was discontent in many areas, especially in La Vendée. Here a peasant uprising against conscription (being forced into the army) was being encouraged by the Church and the landowners. Added to this there was a sharp rise in the price of bread, and in parts of Paris the workers were looting bakeries.

This desperate situation called for desperate remedies. The defence of France was more important than anything else. Many people felt that in this time of crisis a strong government was needed more than liberty and equality. One of the middle-class political 'clubs', called the Jacobins, promised this strong leadership.

The Jacobins were tough, ruthless men who were more willing than other middle-class politicians to consider severe measures. They were also prepared to work with the ordinary people of Paris. In the summer of 1793 the Jacobins seized power and established a virtual dictatorship. France was now to be governed by two committees – the Committee of Public Safety and the Committee of General Security.

The Terror

The Jacobin dictatorship made tough new laws. Every man, woman and child was ordered to help with the war effort; prices and wages were fixed by law; BLACK MARKETEERS, SPECULATORS, DEFEATISTS and spies were rounded up and imprisoned. People who broke the new laws could expect the ultimate penalty – death. The Convention declared: 'Let Terror be the order of the day'.

The Revolutionary Tribunal

People suspected of crimes against the Revolution were tried by a Revolutionary Tribunal. In every part of France Revolutionary Vigilance Committees (see Source 24) were set up to draft lists of suspects and to issue warrants for their arrest. Some suspects were guilty of nothing more than 'indifference' to the Revolution. Some of the charges were ridiculous. A young army volunteer, Gabriel David, was found guilty of writing

SOURCE 24 A Revolutionary Vigilance Committee at work

'infamous words' and was imprisoned. He had written 'Shit on the nation' on his leave pass.

Source 25 is an extract from the Law of Suspects of September 1793. It gives some idea of the sort of people the Vigilance Committees were supposed to investigate.

SOURCE 25

The following are considered suspected persons: first, those who by their behaviour, the company they keep, their talk or writings have shown themselves to be supporters of tyranny; secondly, those who do not earn an honest living or perform their public duties; thirdly, those who have been refused certificates of patriotism; fourthly, public officials suspended or dismissed by the National Convention; fifthly, those former nobles . . . who have not steadily shown their loyalty to the Revolution.

M. de Kerverseau, a resident of Paris during the Terror, described one of these Committees (Source 26).

SOURCE 26

There was the same stench, the same bunch of brigands. . . . They wore the rags of pretended poverty but they had hearts of steel and the manner of tyrants. At that time in Paris dirtiness was a sort of passport . . . long, dirty beards, greasy, filthy hair, stockings with holes, worn-out shoes, red hats, ragged coats, hands sticky with filth, shirts open to the waist.

1 Look at Source 24.
  a What emotions are reflected in the faces of the Committee members?
  b Do you think the suspect on the left had much hope of a fair hearing?
  c How far does this picture agree with de Kerverseau's description of a Revolutionary Vigilance Committee?

2 What words and phrases in Source 26 make it clear that de Kerverseau disliked the Vigilance Committees and the people who worked on them?

ACTIVITY

The Vigilance Committee

The best way to try to understand the confusion and fear felt by people at the time of the Terror is to put yourself in the position of one of the accused suspects. Divide into groups of seven or eight.

1 In each group four of you must play the part of the Vigilance Committee. It is your job to write the charges against the accused and to interrogate them when they are brought before you. Remember that you have a deep hatred of all counter-revolutionaries. You are determined to wipe out all enemies of 'virtue'. You are on the look-out for hoarders, speculators, defeatists, cowards and people who have not been active enough in supporting the Revolution.

2 The rest of each group are the suspects. You have been arrested and imprisoned. It is now early morning and you will be hauled before the Vigilance Committee in just 20 minutes' time.
  a Each suspect must prepare a general statement to be read out before the Vigilance Committee. It must state how loyal you are to the Republic and say why you think the Revolution has benefited France. Remember, your life depends on how sincere you make this statement sound. You can help each other with your statements if you like.
  b You must also think of a good story to tell the Vigilance Committee about your alleged crime. It is almost certain that a neighbour has informed on you but you cannot be sure what the charge against you will be. Perhaps you really are loyal to the Revolution and the whole thing has been a terrible mistake — they have arrested the wrong person. It should be easy enough to prove your innocence by giving an account of all the good work you have done for the Revolution. Or perhaps you are guilty of counter-revolutionary crimes — of hoarding bread, criticising the government, or not cheering loudly enough at revolutionary meetings.

3 At the end of twenty minutes, each suspect must appear in turn before the Vigilance Committee. After the statements, charges and denials have been heard, a verdict must be passed. This may be death by guillotine.

The guillotine

In this new age of equality a single method of execution for both rich and poor was invented (see Source 27). Previously, execution had been by sword or axe for nobles and hanging or breaking on the wheel for others. Now everyone sentenced to death was guillotined (see Sources 28 and 29).

SOURCE 27

The National Assembly considering . . . that humanity requires that the death penalty be as painless as possible decrees that . . . decapitation [beheading] be carried out according to the method approved by the permanent secretary of the Academy of Surgery.

SOURCE 28 A reluctant victim is prepared for execution.

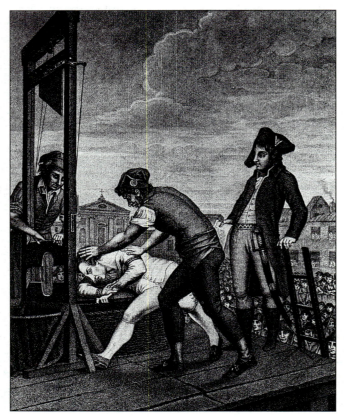

SOURCE 29

As the guillotine was always ready a quarter of an hour before the arrival of the condemned, one of the assistants who had been helping to set it up amused himself by dancing round the instrument and by his capers, antics and grimaces entertained the crowd! But the highlight was the 'amputation' [cutting off] of heads which, severed by the blade of the guillotine, fell speedily on top of one another into a kind of basin where they floated in blood, which splashed up as the heads dropped and flooded the pavement.

M. de Kerverseau

SOURCE 30

Executions from April to July, 1794

	Nobles	Upper middle class	Lower middle class	Clergy	Working class (Towns)	Peasants	Total
April	111	165	50	90	309	315	1099
May	124	186	113	54	172	107	780
June	160	277	168	123	321	95	1157
July	341	349	165	204	214	100	1397
Total	736	977	496	471	1016	617	4433

1 Most people think of the guillotine as a terrifying, cruel method of execution. Was this the intention of the National Assembly when they introduced it? (Source 27)

2 A joke of the time described the guillotine as 'the best doctor'. What was meant by this?

3 Look at the table of executions in Source 30.

   a When does the Terror seem to have been at its height?

   b Considering that the Revolution began as an attack on the aristocracy and the Church, what do you find surprising about these figures?

   c Using graph paper, with the months on the horizontal axis and the number of deaths on the vertical axis, produce a graph showing the number of executions by social class between April and July 1794. You could use a different colour line for each class.

The Importance of the French Revolution

Some historians have seen the Terror as the first example of a modern POLICE STATE. Certainly it provided a terrible warning of what can happen when extremists and fanatics get into power. But this was not the only legacy of the French Revolution. It also launched two new forces into the world — nationalism (looked at in Unit 4) and democracy (dealt with in Unit 5).

'Nationalism' means the desire of people of the same race, creed, culture and language to be a united, independent nation. It can also mean a belief that your nation is better than any other. Of course, the French Revolution did not deliberately set out to encourage a sense of nationalism in the people of Europe. However, France's wars with the rest of Europe had this accidental effect. By June 1794 the foreign invasions of France had been halted and the French armies now moved to the attack. Over the next twenty years the French armies conquered much of Europe. The defeated countries grew to hate French military occupation with its demands for taxes and soldiers for the army. They began to discover their own national characters in their resistance to France.

'Democracy' means rule by the people. The French Revolution threw up many democratic ideas about brotherhood, liberty and equality. For a short time in 1793, there was even a democratic constitution in France which granted the vote to all adult males and gave them considerable control over their representatives and governors. However, the state of national emergency at that time meant that the constitution was never actually applied. Democracy remained a dream which the French revolutionaries struggled for but never quite achieved. It was a dream which they left for future generations.

ASSESSMENT

Empathy

1 Many of the men who were responsible for the Terror were the same men who had supported the Declaration of the Rights of Man. Imagine that you are one of these men. Write a speech justifying your support for the Terror.

Cause and consequence

2 Why do you think the French Revolution resulted in the Terror? Write your reasons in order of importance.

Investigation

1 It is estimated that about 40,000 people were executed during the Terror. Try to find out how this compares with more recent 'Terrors' — for example, Joseph Stalin's purges in 1930s Russia or the Nazi persecution of the Jews in Europe in the 1930s and 1940s.

2 Are there any parts of the world today where governments are attempting to control people by terror? Look at newspapers and Amnesty International pamphlets.

3

The changing role of women

SOURCE 1

I was then surrounded and forced back on to the chair, which was tilted backwards. While I was held down, a nasal tube was inserted. It is two yards long, with a funnel at the end. The end is put up the left and right nostril on alternate days. The sensation is most painful – the drums of the ears seem to be bursting and there is a horrible pain in the throat and the breast. The tube is pushed down twenty inches. The one holding the funnel end pours the liquid down – about a pint of milk, mixed with egg. The after-effects are a feeling of faintness and a great pain in the breast, nose and ears. I was sick on the first occasion.

Mary Leigh, 1912, quoted in BBC, *Shoulder to Shoulder*

SOURCE 1 WAS written by Mary Leigh. It sounds as though she was being tortured. In fact, she was being force-fed (see Source 2). She was on a hunger-strike because she, like many other women, had been imprisoned for her activities with a group of women called 'Suffragettes'. They were active in Britain between the 1890s and 1914. Their campaign had the simple slogan 'Votes for Women'. The Suffragettes thought that one important way in which the status of women in society could, and should, be improved was

SOURCE 2 A Suffragette is force-fed in prison, 1909

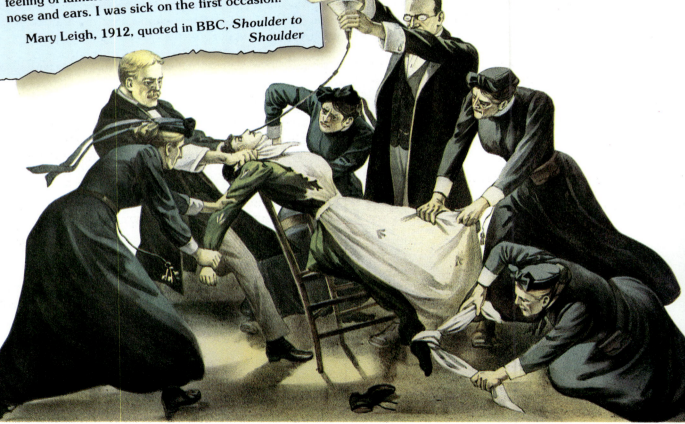

for women to have some say in the process of electing MPs to Parliament. When peaceful meetings, protests and petitions were ignored, they deliberately set out to win attention by chaining themselves to railings, by smashing windows and by setting fire to empty houses (see Source 3).

Source 4 shows Margaret Thatcher in 1979, just after she had become Britain's first woman Prime Minister. For this event to happen a massive change must have taken place in British society. How many Suffragettes of eighty years ago — a few of whom are still alive today —

SOURCE 3 A Suffragette is arrested outside Buckingham Palace, 1914

SOURCE 4 Mrs Thatcher in 1979 with members of her Cabinet

would have foreseen the day when a woman would hold the most powerful and important job in the land?

But this does not mean that the struggle for women's rights is now over. There are still relatively few women Members of Parliament, and women remain in a small minority in the leading professions like law, accountancy and medicine. Many women claim that men continue to rule the home and family. Moreover, in some parts of the world the role of women has hardly changed at all in the last hundred years.

1 **Why, do you think, the prison authorities chose to force-feed the woman in Source 2 rather than releasing her or letting her starve herself to death?**

2 **Look at Source 4. Does the fact that Margaret Thatcher became Prime Minister of Britain prove that the Suffragette campaign was successful? Can you think of any other reasons why women were finally granted the vote? (Look ahead to Sources 5 to 16 for help with this question.)**

AIMS

This unit looks at how women's role in society has changed. It asks you to think about all of the following:

- different rates of change
- different causes of change
- the reasons for lack of change
- the effects of change on women's lifestyles
- the effects of change on society in general

It is not possible to study the picture worldwide. This unit concentrates on just two countries: Britain and China. By doing so it provides a contrast between Western and Eastern attitudes, and between capitalist and Communist approaches. You will be able to see similarities as well as differences between the two countries.

Over the last 100 years, many different factors have helped change British women's lives. We are going to look at seven of them.

In each case, you will need to try to understand what *caused* the change. You will also need to understand the *effects* of the change. A good way of looking at the effects of change is through pictures. If you compare a picture from an earlier date with one from a later date, you can often see a clear difference.

SOURCE 5 A Suffragette rally in London, 1908

SOURCE 6 A 'Women's Lib' march in the 1970s

Factor 1: Organised campaigns by women for reform

- In 1903 Mrs Emmeline Pankhurst founded the Women's Social and Political Union in Manchester.

- She and her fellow Suffragettes set about winning 'votes for women'.

- When peaceful protests did not work, they set out to get attention in any way they could.

- In 1918 the vote was granted to women over 30.

- In 1928 the vote was granted to women over 21.

- In the late 1960s the Women's Liberation Movement was founded.

- It wanted to make women equal to men in all ways.

- It claimed that women were still not treated fairly — there was still DISCRIMINATION against women in schools, in jobs and in the home.

- Supporters of 'Womens Lib' organised public rallies, published magazines and newspapers, and put pressure on MPs to change laws that discriminated against women.

Discuss in pairs.

1 Suffragettes broke the law to draw attention to their cause. Do you think they were right to do so?

2 Some people argue that the Suffragettes' violent methods actually stopped them from winning the vote sooner. Their actions convinced men that women weren't fit to vote. What do you think about this argument?

3 The Women's Liberation Movement in the 1970s did not resort to violent tactics. Why do you think this was?

Factor 2: Improved contraception

- In 1860 over half of the families in England and Wales had five or more children.

- In 1890, working-class wives spent, on average, 15 years either pregnant or looking after a child under one year old.

- In 1877 Charles Bradlaugh and Annie Besant were prosecuted for publishing a book giving details of birth control.

- In 1921 Marie Stopes opened a family planning clinic in London giving free advice and cheap contraceptives.

- By 1930 the Family Planning Association had been formed. National birth control clinics were started around the country. Every local authority was obliged to have them by 1967.

- In the 1960s the contraceptive pill was introduced. This meant that women could control the size of their families even more easily.

- On average, a British family today has 2.2 children.

1 Victorian families were large. Who would have faced the bigger problems — working-class women or upper-class women? Why?

2 Women now have the 'freedom' to choose how many children they have (unless their religion forbids contraception). Do you think this is an important freedom? Why?

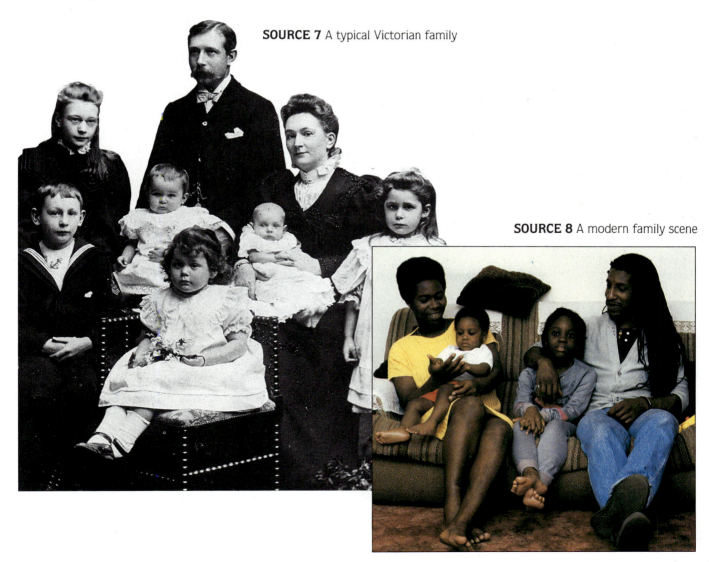

SOURCE 7 A typical Victorian family

SOURCE 8 A modern family scene

Factor 3: Improvements in education for girls

- Victorian girls from wealthy families did go to school but they were not taught 'difficult' subjects like mathematics and science.

- They learned the skills necessary to attract a husband – singing, playing the piano, painting and 'the art of conversation'.

- In the 1880s and 1890s 5–12-year-old girls from poorer families started to go to school. (There were still not enough schools for everyone.) In the schools, girls learnt only the basics of reading, writing and arithmetic. They also learnt how to cook and sew, so that they could become good wives and mothers.

- In the 1850s Frances and Dorothea Beale set up girls' schools which taught the same subjects as those taught to boys, including science.

- In 1866 Dr Elizabeth Garrett overcame huge difficulties to become the first fully qualified female doctor in Britain.

- Today girls can study the same subjects as boys. However, fewer girls than boys choose to study science and mathematics. There are therefore more male scientists and mathematicians.

SOURCE 9 Girls at school in 1885

SOURCE 10 Girls in a science lesson in the 1980s

1 Do you think that Elizabeth Garrett becoming a doctor was an important event? Why?

2 Why do you think some girls today are not interested in maths and science?

3 Do you think it's important that girls have the *opportunity* to study the same subjects as boys, and to study them to the same level? Why?

Factor 4: The two World Wars

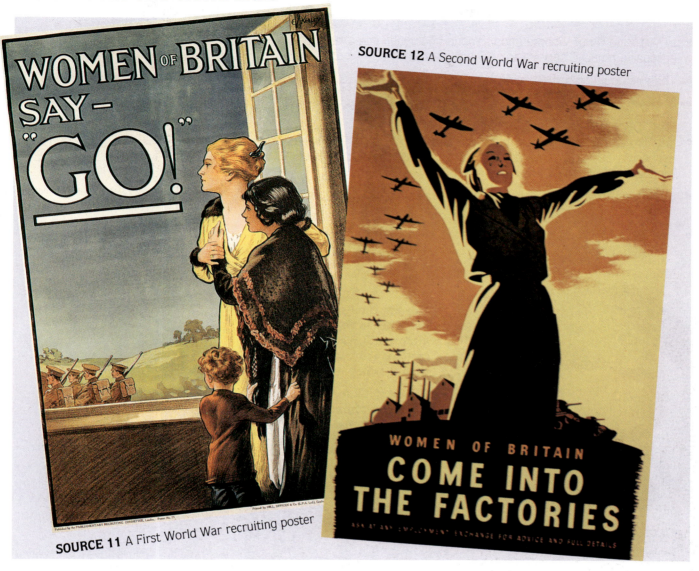

SOURCE 11 A First World War recruiting poster

SOURCE 12 A Second World War recruiting poster

- People thought the First World War would only last a short while. Women would stay quietly at home and await their husband's return.

- The war lasted over 4 years. More and more men were recruited into the army. More and more women were needed to take over their jobs.

- Women, for the first time, became railway porters, van drivers and general labourers.

- For many women, it was the first time they had ever worked outside the home. They discovered a new independence.

- During the Second World War the government called up women to work in factories, to manage farms and run transport services.

- Although women did the same jobs as men, they did not receive the same pay. It was several years before they won equal pay.

1 Look at Source 11. What does this say about a woman's role in times of war?

2 Look at Source 12. What does this say about a woman's role in times of war?

3 Do you think it was easier for changes to take place when a war was going on? Why? Were these changes bound to last?

Factor 5: New labour-saving machines in the home

- In Victorian times women had to spend hours cleaning, washing and preparing meals. There were no machines to help.

- The rich could afford domestic servants.

- The poor might have to do all the chores in the home as well as working up to 12 hours a day in a factory.

- Vacuum cleaners were invented in the nineteenth century but were very expensive. By 1930 they cost one tenth of what they did in 1906. Even the less well-off could afford them.

- Nowadays most homes have vacuum cleaners, washing machines, electric irons, electric cookers, fridges, freezers and sewing machines.

- Housework today can be done more quickly and efficiently than in Victorian times.

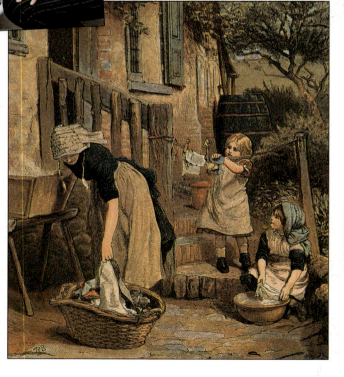

> 1 Why are time-saving machines in the home important? What can women (and men) do with the extra time they now have?
>
> 2 Do you think men nowadays help more around the house? Why should they or shouldn't they?

SOURCE 14
Washday in the 1980s: machines do the work

SOURCE 13
Washday in the 1880s: hard manual work

Factor 6: New laws protecting the rights of women

- In 1792 Mary Wollstonecraft wrote a book called *Vindication of the Rights of Women*. She claimed that the laws of England treated women like an inferior race. A wife was her husband's property. He owned her belongings, her earnings and her children.

- In 1857 a law was passed allowing a woman to divorce her husband without needing a special Act of Parliament. This also gave a separated wife the right to see her children.

- After 1881 a married woman was legally able to own property.

- Over the last hundred years a number of laws have been passed giving women the same legal rights as men.

- In 1970 the Equal Pay Act made it illegal to pay women and men different wages for doing the same or similar work.

- In 1975 the Sex Discrimination Act was passed. This made it illegal to discriminate against women (or men) in education, jobs, housing or services.

- Some employers have found ways of getting round these Acts. Women or men who feel 'cheated' can ask for their case to be heard in court.

> Do you think laws are a good way of bringing about change? What can laws *not* change?

Factor 7: New machines at work

- During the Industrial Revolution (Unit 1) new machines were invented which were well suited to women's skills. Women could operate spinning machines and power looms well.

- In the 1860s the typewriter was invented, and in 1876 the telephone. Operating these machines again required skill rather than strength.

- By 1911 there were nearly 120,000 women in Britain working as clerks or telephone operators.

- Over the last 10–15 years, computer technology has opened up new jobs. Women are employed both in assembling computers and in using them.

- Most secretarial and clerical jobs are done by women. The work can be monotonous and is not always well paid.

SOURCE 16 Women computer operators, 1980s

SOURCE 15 Women telephonists at a London exchange, 1883

1 Why do you think that women rather than men are nowadays employed for typing, operating telephone exchanges and assembling computer equipment?

2 Why do jobs employing mainly women still often pay lower wages?

ASSESSMENT

Change

1 Pick out the *two* factors which you think have been most important in changing women's lives. Explain your choice.

Role of the individual

2 Look back at Source 4. Do you think the achievements of individual women have been important in bringing about change?

Change

3 The changes which have taken place over the last hundred years have not just affected women. Write three or four sentences explaining how the changes have affected each of the following:
a family life
b men's views and attitudes
c the workplace
d government.

WOMEN IN CHINA

Since 1949 China has been a COMMUNIST state. One principle of Communism is that all people should be treated as equal. Before the Communist Revolution, women did not play an equal part in Chinese society. Since 1949, the Communist government has passed laws which have changed the lives of millions of Chinese women.

As you read through this section, look for:

a) How the rapid changes have affected Chinese women, and Chinese society in general.

b) Any aspects of life where the old views of women do not seem to have changed.

c) Similarities and differences between the changes in China and those in Britain.

Women in China before 1949

Before the Communist Revolution of 1949, women were treated very much as the inferior sex. One of the things they had to suffer was footbinding. Men liked women with small feet and footbinding produced small feet (see Source 17). Qui Ju described what happened (Source 18).

SOURCE 18

Before many years have passed, they take out a pair of snow-white bands and bind them around our feet. They tighten them with strips of white cotton. Even when we go to bed at night we are not allowed to loosen them. The result is that the flesh peels away and the bones bend and buckle under.

BBC2, 1986

At the age of 14 or 15 a girl might be married off. The husband was chosen by her parents and by a matchmaker. Once married, she went to live with her husband and his family. She was hardly ever allowed out of the home. Her job was to work in the home and produce children.

Women were under a lot of pressure to produce sons. Baby girls were seen as just an extra mouth to feed. Many of them were killed at birth.

SOURCE 17 Young and old in China. Notice the size of the old woman's feet.

Women in China since 1949

When the Chinese government of Mao Zedong gained power in 1949, it introduced a series of reforms, as shown in Sources 19, 20 and 21.

SOURCE 20

Mao also banned other horrible practices such as the drowning of newborn female babies, polygamy [having more than one wife] and the selling of women as servants or prostitutes.

Chow Qingli

SOURCE 19

1950 Communist Marriage Law

Article 3: Marriage shall be based upon the complete willingness of the two parties. Neither party shall use compulsion and no party shall be allowed to interfere.

Article 9: Both husband and wife shall have equal rights in the possession and management of family property.

SOURCE 21

We advocate [actively support] equal rights for husband and wife. We oppose the idea that man is superior to woman or that the husband has special powers over his wife. We oppose all discrimination or ill-treatment of the wife.

China Youth Daily, 1950

SOURCE 22 Men and women at work on equal terms

SOURCE 23 A state-run crèche in China, 1980

Mao was determined to modernise China. He saw that women were a 'vast reserve of labour power'. He believed that they should be set to work and should receive equal pay for equal work (see Source 22).

Soon all Chinese women had a job. Those who had children left them at schools or state-run nurseries (see Source 23).

All these changes did bring some problems. A report produced by the Minority Rights Group in 1982 said that women now had to carry a 'double burden': they had to work both inside and outside the home.

1 **Who might not have been in favour of the new Communist Marriage Law?**

2 **Why did Mao encourage women to go out to work?**

Family planning

Women's lives have also been changed by government family planning programmes. In China, each married couple is encouraged to have just one child. Contraception can be obtained easily — and so can abortions. The government justifies this policy by saying that Chinese people will never be better off unless the growth of the Chinese population can be stopped or reversed.

SOURCE 24 The Family Planning Campaign never stops

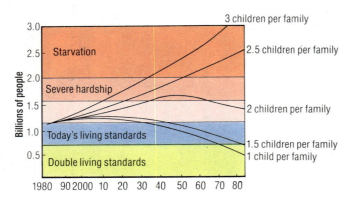

SOURCE 25 How China's population could grow

Source 25 shows how China's population could grow over the next hundred years. The rate varies according to how many children each family has.

> 1 What is China's population today?
>
> 2 How big would the population be by the year 2080 if families had three children each? Would they be suffering poverty, hardship or starvation?
>
> 3 What would happen to the population by the year 2080 if families had only one child each? Would they be better off than they are today?

Mrs Tian, who works as a family planning officer, explained the rewards for those who sign the one-child policy (Source 26).

SOURCE 26

For those who agree, there is a package of rewards. There is a monthly bonus of five yuan [about £2] for each parent until the child is 14. The child will also get the best schooling, and the parents the right to better housing. Each brigade [neighbourhood unit] has women officials who keep an eye on the women and look out for any signs of pregnancy. There is no room for personal freedom on such an important issue.

China's Child, *BBC2, 1984*

Mrs Chang, another family planning officer, described what happened when a woman wanted to have a second baby without permission (Source 27).

SOURCE 27

When we started trying to change her mind she was seven months pregnant. I was very worried seeing her get bigger and bigger. The leaders of the commune all came to persuade her. We thought it would be best for her if she had an abortion, but at first she would not agree. . . . In the end I talked her round.

China's Child, *BBC2, 1984*

The one-child policy has not done away with the age-old practice of infanticide (killing newborn babies). A boy is still felt to be more valuable than a girl, and baby girls are sometimes killed at birth so that parents can try again for a boy (see Source 28).

SOURCE 28

There are five times as many male as female babies alive. In one village more than forty babies had been drowned in the past two years. In another village, eight babies had been born in the last year – three boys were still alive, three girls had been drowned and two abandoned. Unknown numbers of women had been beaten by their husbands for giving birth to a girl instead of a boy.

One Village in China, BBC 2, 1987

The one-child policy may seem harsh to us, but in the past Chinese women often had to find their own equally harsh solution to having too many mouths to feed (see Source 29).

1 Look at Sources 26 and 27. How does the government try to make sure that its one-child policy is successful? List three or four things it does.

2 Look at Sources 25 and 29. Do you think the government is justified in forcing families to agree to its one-child policy? Explain your answer carefully.

Chinese society is still changing a great deal. Since Mao's death in 1976 China's leaders have been more ready to look for friendship and trade with countries in the West. Western goods, like washing machines and freezers, are now on sale in some Chinese stores. Some Western fashions have been taken up (see Source 30).

These changes in society may in the future bring about further dramatic changes in Chinese women's lives.

SOURCE 30 East meets West in modern China

ASSESSMENT

Similarity and difference	**1a** Does the government seem to have played a more important role in changing women's lives in China than in Britain? **b** Can you explain this difference?
Similarity and difference	**2** Both China and Britain have family planning and free contraception. Who decides on family size in Britain? Who decides in China? Has contraception 'freed' Chinese women in the same way as it has British women? Explain your answer carefully.
Similarity and difference	**3** Look back at Source 22. **a** Do you see women in Britain working alongside men like this? **b** Do you think women should do jobs which need hard, physical work if they want to be seen as equal?
Utility	**4** Do you think Source 22 can be used as evidence that women in China are now more equal with men than women in Britain are? Explain your answer carefully.

4

Nationalism

SOURCE 1 A Nazi rally in the 1930s

SOURCE 1 SHOWS a huge German crowd at a Nazi rally in 1938. Thousands of men and women, young and old, have come to see their leader, Adolf Hitler. They all salute the procession as it enters the stadium.

And Hitler did not disappoint them. Source 2 shows just what a dramatic speechmaker he was. William Shirer, an American journalist, witnessed the Nuremberg Rally of 1934 (see Source 3).

SOURCE 3

'We are strong and we will get stronger', Hitler shouted at them through the microphone, his words echoing across the hushed field from the loudspeakers. And there, in the floodlit night, jammed together like sardines, in one mass formation . . . the little men of Germany . . . were merged completely.

William Shirer, *Berlin Diary*

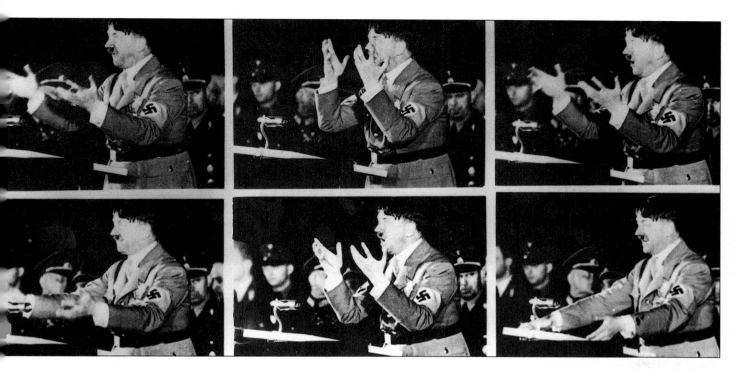

SOURCE 2 The Führer at work — notice the style and power of his speechmaking

Everyone in the crowd felt a strong loyalty towards Hitler. He aroused their emotions. He made them believe in him, in themselves and in their country.

---

1 **Divide into small groups of four or five and explore what you think is meant by loyalty.**
 • **Each think of one thing that you are loyal towards.**
 • **How *strong* is your loyalty to whatever you have selected? How far would you go to support whatever it is you are loyal towards?**
 • **Share your ideas with others in your group.**

2 **Get together as a class and explore the ways in which people show loyalty in Britain.**
 • **What are they loyal towards? — the Queen?, the government?, the country, or what?**
 • **When do people feel most strongly about loyalty to their country? — at sporting events?, on holiday abroad?, at times of war?, or when?**
 • **Think of examples in Britain's past when people's 'national' loyalties were stirred. How did people's NATIONALISM show itself?**

AIMS

This unit is about nationalism — the strong loyalty of people towards their own country. Sometimes this loyalty is accompanied by a dislike of other countries and their peoples. This century, nationalism has been a major force in shaping events all over the world.

In this unit we shall focus on Germany. You will follow its ups and downs, exploring the part that nationalism has played in its eventful history.

Much of the information will be presented to you through the eyes and ears of just one German family — the Gross family in Berlin, who have a small shoemaking business. You will be trying to understand past events through EMPATHY. You will be asked to understand the hopes and fears of the Gross family, and you will try to see things as they saw them.

In this way you will be looking at the events which led up to the Second World War through the eyes of ordinary Germans living at the time, rather than British people living several decades later.

The unit ends with a brief look at a more recent event — the Falklands War — where nationalism may also have played a part.

EXPLORING NATIONALISM IN GERMANY

This section is divided into two parts. The first consists of a Fact File on key events in German history since 1870.

The second part consists of 'flashbacks' into the lives of the Gross family at three significant dates — 1923, 1936 and 1945. Each flashback is written in playscript form. Although the family is imaginary, the times in which the flashbacks are set are real. The Sources are all real and the events mentioned did happen. [Details of the Sources are given in the Lesson Notes.]

GERMANY: Fact File

Before 1871 'Germany' did not exist as a united nation. 'Germany' was simply a geographical term to describe a particular area of Europe peopled by millions who spoke a common language. Today two separate, independent and powerful German nations exist. What has happened since 1871 is a story of major events and changes. These changes are shown in the maps.

For much of the 19th century Germany was made up of independent states of varying size and power. In the 1860s Otto von Bismarck masterminded the expansion of one state called Prussia. After a series of political and military successes this led, in stages, to the creation of a united nation. In 1871 the German Empire was proclaimed, with Wilhelm I as its 'Kaiser' (Emperor).

In the last 30 years of the 19th century, Germany developed its economic and military power. By 1900 Germany was one of the strongest countries in Europe and felt ready to challenge Europe's main powers — Britain, France and Russia.

In 1914, after a complicated series of diplomatic events, Germany — led by Kaiser Wilhelm II — found itself involved in what we now call the First World War. At the time, it was called the Great War. Germany fought in western Europe against Britain, France and Italy, and in eastern Europe against Russia.

Following Germany's defeat in the First World War the Kaiser fled. Germany became a republic and set up a shaky but DEMOCRATIC GOVERNMENT. This government — the Weimar Republic — faced many serious problems (see Flashback 1923). The problems were both political and economic, including spectacular INFLATION. Many of the problems resulted from the Treaty of Versailles — the harsh peace treaty which Germany had been forced to sign after the First World War.

Serious economic problems between 1928 and 1933 made possible the rise of the Nazi Party led by Adolf Hitler. After gaining power in 1933 Hitler dominated Germany as its Führer (leader) and promised that his

1914: Before the First World War

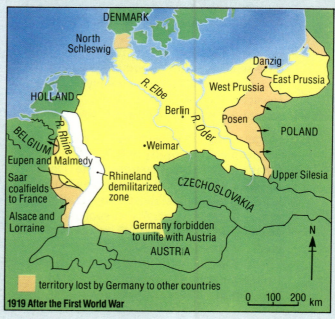

1919 After the First World War

territory lost by Germany to other countries

new, prosperous and powerful German Reich (empire) would last for a 1000 years. In the 12 years it did last many aspects of German life were changed (see Flashback 1936) because of Hitler's dictatorship and his one-party state.

Some of Hitler's ideas and actions led to the Second World War (1939–1945). Once again, German forces fought right across Europe. After winning early victories, the Germans were totally defeated by 1945 (see Flashback 1945). For a time Germany was run by the victorious Allied nations, but as Russia and America/Britain/France found it difficult to work together, Germany became split into two. (See Unit 7: Superpower Conflict.)

In 1949 the two separate countries of East and West Germany were set up. Since then, both have developed in different political and economic ways. East Germany is a Communist state closely connected with the USSR. West Germany is a thriving democracy with a high standard of living which looks to Western Europe and North America for friendship (see Unit 5: Democracy).

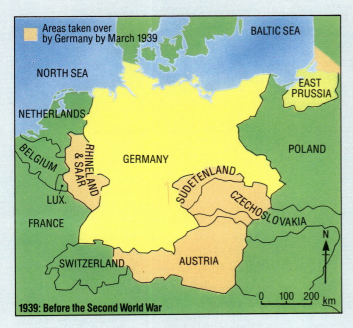

1939: Before the Second World War

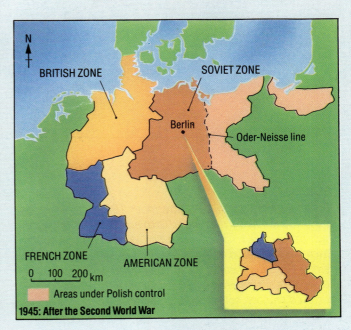

1945: After the Second World War

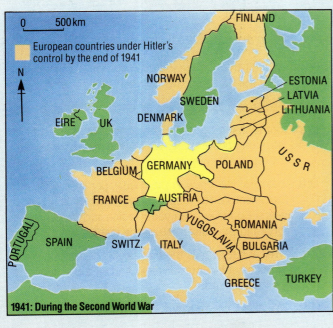

1941: During the Second World War

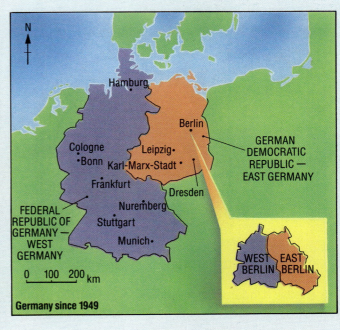

Germany since 1949

FLASHBACK 1923

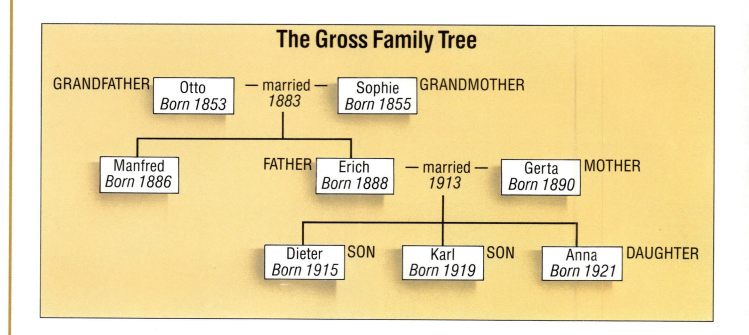

The Gross Family Tree

GRANDFATHER | Otto *Born 1853* — married 1883 — Sophie *Born 1855* | GRANDMOTHER

Manfred *Born 1886*

FATHER | Erich *Born 1888* — married 1913 — Gerta *Born 1890* | MOTHER

Dieter *Born 1915* SON | Karl *Born 1919* SON | Anna *Born 1921* DAUGHTER

SCENE ONE

It is late afternoon on 11th November 1923. The scene is the Gross family's living room. Otto and Erich sit opposite each other close to a weak coal fire, deep in conversation. Erich has a tattered diary on his lap. Sophie is preparing the family's evening meal in the kitchen. Anna is asleep in her cot. Karl is sitting on the carpet playing with a box of battered wooden soldier figures. Dieter is shortly to arrive home from school. Gerta will be back later from her office job.

As the daylight fades, an air of gloom hangs over the scene.

Erich: Just think . . . 5 years ago today . . . the end of the Great War.

He turns in his battered diary to an entry he wrote in November 1918.

Erich: *November 9th:* The Kaiser is supposed to
(reads)   have ABDICATED. Our splendid Germany
SOURCE 4   has fallen to pieces!
November 11th: The war is over. We looked forward to this moment as the most splendid event of our lives; and now, humbled, torn and bleeding, we've surrendered.

Listen to this final order from my General:

(reads): Undefeated by the enemy, we have to
SOURCE 5   abandon the territory which we occupied.

We can march back to our beloved country with heads held high. Keep the German Army's honour to the last, and then, in spite of the unhappy end, you will be able to look back full of pride, to the very end of your days, upon your heroic deeds.

Otto: I blame backsliders and defeatists at home for Germany's collapse.

Erich: Don't speak to me of them — nor the treacherous Communists.

Karl begins to make war-like noises.

Erich: When I think of what sort of country Germany is now for Karl to grow up in — it fills me with rage!

Otto: Patience — look, already he is learning to go to war!

Erich Some chance! Not in a Germany crippled by that shameful peace treaty which was meekly accepted by our feeble new leaders.

Otto: Leaders! Ha! I saw in the newspaper that when our president visited Munich he was met by boos and jeers! Good God, can you imagine such a scene greeting the Kaiser before the war?

Erich: Well, what hope is there of people respecting the government — it is so weak! And all those different political parties!

Otto: We didn't need them in the Kaiser's day.

Erich: What Germany needs is her strength, pride and purpose back again. But will I live to see it?

The door opens and Dieter appears. He has just come in from school.

Dieter: Hello Father, Grandfather. Karl, what are you up to?

Karl: I'm playing soldiers.

Dieter: Oh, yes, that reminds me — Father, our teacher at school today asked us what we would like to be once we are older. I said a soldier, like you were. She said that would be hard, because we are not allowed to have many soldiers! Is that true?

Erich: Yes, Dieter. At the moment.

Dieter: But who says so?

Otto: It's complicated — it was decided upon by the countries who Germany fought against in the Great War.

Dieter: Why should they decide what our country does?

Erich: A good question, my son. But it will not always be so. Germany will rise again, and at its head will be a fine army, with good leaders. And *you* may be in that army, Dieter.

Dieter: Why did Germany lose the Great War, Father?

Otto: Through no fault of the army, Dieter — remember that. Now, no more questions. Go and help your grandmother in the kitchen.

The two men sit in silence, each with his own thoughts, and Dieter departs.

SCENE TWO
The door opens and Gerta returns from work. She is laden with a small bag of groceries and a large holdall full of banknotes.

Gerta: My God, Erich, do you know how long I spent queuing for these? Forty minutes. It's hopeless.

Otto: It's the fault of the French! They are 'creaming off' all Germany's goods! We are crippled by payments to the French — as a punishment for a war we neither started nor lost! That's why you spend ages queuing. Blame it on the French.

Erich: It's not as simple as that, Father.

Otto: Oh, no? Then answer me this. Why, earlier this year, when we couldn't pay the French anymore, did their troops take over the Ruhr? To claim their war booty — by force! My God, when I was a boy — we showed the French what for in 1870! Six weeks — six weeks, that's all it took to destroy the French!

Gerta: And where did that victory get Germany?

Otto: I'll tell you where! It made us into a united country!

Gerta: Yes, yes, but all that's in the past — I don't have time to worry about history. I've got to earn a living to feed us all until Erich here gets some orders for shoes.

Erich: It's not that easy, Gerta! I have tried. Look, how many times have I had handbills printed? These days, people are too busy staying alive — like us — finding food and bartering items to pay for them.

Gerta: It's madness! Now we are paid *twice a day* in the office. I have to rush out at lunchtime to queue for flour. If I leave it until evening either the shops will have sold out, or the price of what remains will have rocketed.

Otto: It cannot go on like this.

Gerta: Have you any banknotes here?

Erich: Yes, I've two or three in this pot.

He rises, finds them and looks at them.

Just think — 1 billion marks! [Source 6] What that could have bought us before the war!

Gerta: Tomorrow, it might buy five loaves of bread — perhaps by then four!

SOURCE 6 A billion mark banknote, 1923

SOURCE 7 Clerks arrive at a Berlin bank to collect the week's wages using laundry baskets, July 1923

SOURCE 8 A street scene, Berlin, 1923

Otto: It's incredible!

Gerta: Well, it's happening – have you seen this photo in the newspaper showing people taking baskets to collect their money from the bank? [Source 7]

Eric turns the pages.

Erich: Look at this! [Source 8] It fills me with rage! A fine officer, with an Iron Cross, reduced to begging in the streets.

Otto: I fear for this nation's fate. In war we were masters of our own destiny – but now – Is there no end to this dark tunnel of shame?

SCENE THREE

It is mid-evening. After a supper of stew and bread the children have all gone to bed. The four adults sit by the fireside. Sophie is sewing. Erich is reading the newspaper. He reads this report from it.

Erich: Reports of an uprising in Bavaria! An
(reads) attempt to overthrow the government by
SOURCE 9 marching on Berlin has been foiled in Munich. The so-called 'national revolution' began when armed supporters of Adolf Hitler's Nazi Party arrived to take over a political meeting.

An eye-witness said, 'There was a movement at the entrance and eventually steel helmets came into sight. I saw Hitler emerge between two armed soldiers. He climbed on to a chair on my left. He made a sign to the man on his right who fired a shot at the ceiling. Hitler called out "The national revolution has broken out. The hall is surrounded." Then, General Ludendorff, the war hero, who was in on the plot, entered the hall and announced that he too supported the revolution.

Hitler told the crowd, "Now I am going to carry out the vow I made five years ago: to neither rest nor sleep until on the ruins of the pitiful Germany of today has risen a Germany of power and greatness."'

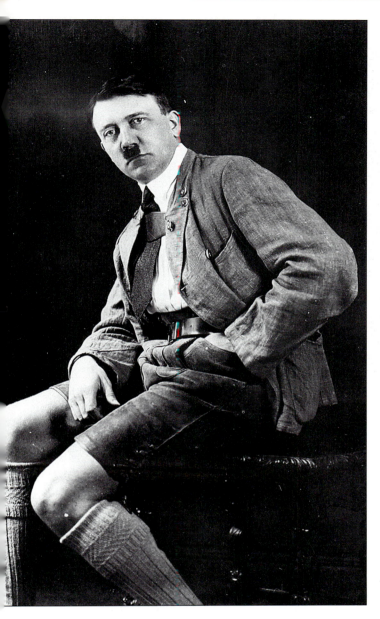

SOURCE 10 Hitler in 1923, appearing as a thoughtful political leader

Meanwhile Hitler's STORMTROOPERS took control of key government buildings in Munich and arrested officials.

The next morning, the 9th, their plans went wrong. Bavarian leaders who had earlier promised to support Hitler changed their minds and ordered the army to attack. Sixteen Nazis were killed. At first, Hitler escaped but later both he and General Ludendorff were arrested. They have been removed to prison to await trial on charges of high treason.

Gerta: Have you heard of Herr Hitler?

Erich: Yes. He fought in the Great War, didn't he?

Otto: Yes. I only know a little about him — just the odd story in the newspaper about his political party.

Sophie: Did Hitler actually start the Nazi Party?

Otto: No, but he took it over when it was very small and made *his* ideas *its* ideas.

Gerta: From what I've heard I don't like his methods. Don't his stormtroopers beat up opponents? Why the violence? Why doesn't he seek power through the election system, like anyone else?

Otto: Because Hitler is a man of *action*, unlike our present leaders.

Erich: His ideas are exactly what Germany needs — he says in his speeches that Germany needs a strong, single leader, that the shameful peace treaty should be removed and that Germany is riddled with 'germs' that ruin our nation — like Communists and Jews.

Otto: And what about revenge?

Erich: Yes, Hitler wants that too — and more space for German people to live and work in.

Sophie: All this has a familiar ring to me — it's similar to things said in the days of the Kaiser before the Great War.

Gerta: Yes, and look what that war brought us. We're all still suffering today, five years after it finished.

Otto: Well, right or wrong, now that his 'national revolution' has failed we'll not be hearing of him again — I expect he'll be off to prison after this.

Erich: It's typical of the state we are in. We've no work, worthless money, crippling debts and weak leaders and yet, when someone with real vision appears, with ideas to improve our nation — he's locked away and forgotten about.

ACTIVITY

Reactions to the past

Each person in your group has to consider the reactions of just one member of the Gross family to events in Germany between 1870 and 1923.

Your teacher has a worksheet for you to do this activity with.

FLASHBACK 1936

SCENE ONE

It is Sunday morning, 14th August 1936. The Gross family still live in their house in Berlin. Since 1923 there have been many changes in both their own lives and those of all people in Germany. Both Otto and Sophie are dead. Erich, now 48, had to sell his shoe workshop, but now has a secure job in a boot-making factory. His firm has thrived in the past few years through a large contract to supply boots to the German army. Gerta no longer works. Dieter, now 21, has just joined the growing army. Both Karl, aged 17, and Anna, aged 15, are still at school. Both children spend much of their free time in the organised activities of the Nazi Party. Karl is a member of the Hitler Youth and Anna is in the German Girls' League.

In the living room, on the mantlepiece, are framed photos of the three children (Sources 11, 12 and 13) together with a new wireless set. On the wall hangs a picture of the Führer, Adolf Hitler.

Anna is puzzling over her maths homework. Her mother, Gerta, is tidying up.

Anna: Oh! I don't understand this problem!

Gerta: Is it anything I can help with, Anna? Let me see the question.

(reads): SOURCE 14 'A bomber aircraft on take-off carries 144 bombs, each weighing 10 kilos. The aircraft takes off for Warsaw, international centre of Jews. It drops all the bombs on the town. On take-off with all the bombs on board and a fuel tank containing 1000 kilos of fuel, the aircraft weighed 8 tonnes. When it returns from the crusade, there are still 230 kilos of fuel left. What is the weight of the aircraft when it lands?'

Mm, well, let's work it out together. Do you have a piece of paper? These books are very different from the ones I used when I was at school.

Anna: Surely maths doesn't change that much does it?

Gerta: No. I wasn't thinking of the maths itself, more the ways in which the questions are set.

Anna: I like the problems— they help you make sense of the question — well, usually!

Gerta: Yes, but — Oh, never mind. At least your homework's done now.

Anna: Just in time, I'm due at the German Girls' League Hall in 10 minutes. Where's Karl?

SOURCE 11
Dieter

SOURCE 12
Karl

SOURCE 13 Anna

Gerta: He's upstairs getting ready for his squad's march. They've got to complete 25 kilometres today.

Karl appears in his Hitler Youth uniform.

Gerta: Now — are you sure you've got everything?

Anna: What about the Blood Flag?

Gerta: What's that?

Karl: No, it will be presented to me for safe keeping once we assemble. I am to carry it throughout the march. It is a glory banner from the street-fighting days of the Party back in the '20s. It's a great honour to be selected to carry it. All the boys in my squad swear this oath [Source 15]. Then we march and sing party songs. It's wonderful. Right, Anna. Do you remember the password and motto for Sunday?

SOURCE 15

In the presence of this Blood Flag which represents our Führer I swear to devote all my energies, all my strength, to the saviour of our country, Adolf Hitler. I am willing and ready to give up my life for him, so help me God. One people. One nation. One Führer.

Anna: Password: Adolf Hitler. Motto: Hitler is Germany and Germany is Hitler.

Karl: What are you going to be doing today, Anna?

Anna: We have Gymnastics Drill this morning, then Moral Training, and in the afternoon Sports.

Karl: Let's go then. We'll see you this evening, Mother.

Gerta: Will you be back in time to listen to Dieter's ceremony at Nuremberg?

Karl: Yes, of course, and the Führer's speech that follows.

Karl and Anna depart. Gerta thinks to herself how empty the house seems and how little she sees of her children these days.

SCENE TWO

Erich returns from a morning walk in a nearby park. In his hand he carries a Party leaflet.

Gerta: What have you got there?

Erich: A Party official was giving these out [Source 16].

Gerta: Five marks a week! We could afford that.

Erich: Yes, Volkswagens are 990 marks new.

Gerta: What are the conditions?

Erich reads from the leaflet . . .

Erich: (reads) **SOURCE 17** As of August 1st, the great savings programme for the People's Car — 'Strength Through Joy' — will begin.

1 Each German can become the purchaser of a Volkswagen.
2 The minimum weekly payment will be 5 marks.
3 A Volkswagen for every German — let that be our aim. It shall be our way of saying 'thank you' to the Führer.

Well, it's a thought. Yes, let's start saving. Who would think people like us might own a People's Car! Times have certainly improved! Germany has so much to thank the Führer for. Where are Karl and Anna?

SOURCE 16 'A Volkswagen for every German'. Nazi leaflet, 1939

Gerta: At Party activities. They won't be back until this evening. I sometimes think they care more for the Führer than they do for us!

Erich: That's hardly fair. It's wonderful that they have pride in their nation, a love of their leader and a sense of purpose for the future. You wouldn't want them to grow up in a Germany as *we* knew it after the war — would you?

Gerta: No, of course not. I agree in many ways, but I sometimes feel uneasy — especially with Dieter just joining the army and Karl sure to follow him.

Erich: Look — I have a job now. We are comfortably off, the children are well fed, clothed and happy. We have regained our pride in our nation. The Party cares about the people — we have much to be grateful for. Besides, I don't like to hear you talk this way.

Gerta: Oh! Why not?

Erich: Because it is not *your* job to question the policies of the Party! Nor mine! You should concentrate upon caring for our children. The Führer will take care of us all! Look how much he's achieved in just three years — at home we've discipline, order and pride, and abroad we've won respect.

Gerta: I still don't like some of the things that seem to be going on. Look at this leaflet that the postman delivered [Source 18].

Erich: What's wrong with that? The Führer explained all that in his book, *Mein Kampf*. Look, it's a fact of evolution that we Germans are superior to other races in the world.

Gerta: I'm just concerned about our own children.

Erich: Well, they're proud to be part of the 'Master Race'. Why should we worry about inferior people? You know, you shouldn't let anyone hear you complaining about what is happening — not even Karl and Anna. They might report you to their Hitler Youth leader.

Gerta: That's ridiculous!

Erich: Is it? At the factory I heard of a priest who told a little joke about Hitler to an electrician working in his church. He was arrested by the GESTAPO, tried and sentenced to death!

Gerta goes about her business in silence. She considers the price that German people might have to pay for regaining their pride and prosperity.

SOURCE 18 Nazi PROPAGANDA: 'We peasants are clearing out the muck'. Here a 'good German' removes Jews and Communists

SCENE THREE

It is 9.00 p.m. on Sunday evening. The family are gathered round their 'People's Receiver' wireless. A mood of excitement and pride fills the family's thoughts. Amongst the ranks of thousands of new army recruits is Dieter, their eldest son. The wireless begins its evening broadcast of the Party Rally at Nuremberg.

Radio: Like a Roman emperor Hitler rode into this
SOURCE 19 medieval town at sundown today past wildly cheering Nazis. Tens of thousands of swastika flags. . . . The streets are a sea of brown and black uniforms.

Erich: It must be wonderful to be there! I can imagine the colours, the noise, the excitement.

Karl: They say that in the main arena alone there are 400,000 people. Dieter told me that at their rehearsal hundreds of searchlights shot high into the night sky.

Erich: And there are the torches, the fireworks, the flags and swastikas. It must be an awesome sight.

Gerta: And our son, Dieter, is there, amongst it all.

Karl: What I wouldn't give to join him!

Gerta: Sh— It's beginning.

A wave of applause drowns out the military music.

Karl/Anna: Sieg Heil! Sieg Heil!

The chants are deafening and continue for several minutes. Then, to the sound of massed bands and choirs, new recruits to the army march past the Führer's raised platform. The wireless throbs to the sound of the soldiers' boots.

Erich: Just think — 100,000 new recruits! That's as many as we were allowed in total after the peace treaty — and now the Führer enlists that number at just one ceremony.

Karl: He has shown the world that Germany was shamefully treated after the Great War. The Führer has torn up that hateful treaty. He has said 'We are strong and we shall get stronger'.

Gerta: Listen, you two — it is time for the oath.

Radio: 'I swear by God this sacred oath: I will
SOURCE 20 render unconditional obedience to Adolf Hitler, the Führer of the German nation and people, Supreme Commander of the Armed Forces, and will be ready as a brave soldier to risk my life at any time for this oath.'

The Gross family look at each other with a mixture of pride, awe and excitement.

In awed tones the Deputy Führer, Rudolf Hess, whispers into the microphone.

The Führer will speak, the Führer will speak!

Erich/ *(saluting as they stand)*
Karl/Anna: Heil Hitler! Heil Hitler!

The roar of the crowds fills the living room.

Radio: The most precious possession on Earth
SOURCE 21 is our own people.
 And for this people, and with this people we will struggle and we will fight
 And never slacken
 Never tire
 Never falter
 Never doubt.
 Long live our Movement!
 Long live our People!

The Führer's words are drowned in waves of chanting:

One Nation! One People! One Führer!

SOURCE 22 After the Allied bombing, 1945

It is 9th March 1945. Erich and Anna, who still live in the house, have removed their few remaining belongings to the cellar. Their house, like many neighbouring ones, is in ruins. [See Source 22]. The upper storeys have been badly damaged by night-time air raids by the RAF. In one such raid, last month, Gerta was killed by a falling roof timber. Their only contact with the outside world is their battered old wireless. Dieter has not been heard of for the past two years. He is missing, believed dead, on the Eastern Front in Russia. Karl is in the army. His unit is making desperate attempts to defend the outskirts of Berlin against the advance of the Russian forces. The noise of the Russian artillery can be heard in the distance.

Anna has been out, trying to find water. She wants to leave the city. Erich is dazed.

Anna returns.

Erich: How much did you get?

Anna: Not much — just enough to drink and wash with.

Erich: We need more — to fill up these pots! What if there is another air raid tonight — we need all our containers full!

Anna: What good will that do? Let the house burn like a torch. Let that be an end to it!

Erich: Don't speak so, Anna! The Führer has commanded 'No surrender'. He is himself directing the defence of Berlin. Remember, Karl is one of our defenders.

Anna: The Führer! He hasn't been seen for months! Germany is finished, Father! Our best plan is to pack up and head west. Better to surrender to the Americans than to the Russians.

Erich: But there are millions of refugees on the move — besides. . . .

Their argument is stopped by the sound of a loudspeaker van outside in the street

Loudspeaker van: The commanding officer of Berlin issues the following order:

SOURCE 23 The capital will be defended to the last man and the last bullet. It is a condition for the successful defence of Berlin that every building, every house, every floor, every hedge, every shell-crater, be defended to the utmost.

Erich: Right, there's an end to this talk of leaving! We will, like our Führer, await our fate! To think it would come to this.

Anna: I don't know why you still have faith in Hitler! Twice in your own lifetime you have seen Germany ruined — because of the aggression of its leaders — yet you still support the man who has brought us into this hell.

Erich: I care for Germany. Its farms, factories and buildings may be in ruins — its people starving, mourning and frightened — but our spirit as a nation will not be defeated. Whenever this war ends, the German people will rebuild.

Anna: But, when that time comes we should not do it with our eyes closed to other nations. We must look to co-operate. We must learn from the lessons of Germany's defeats.

ACTIVITY

Different views

1 **In pairs, discuss the differences in the views of Anna and Erich towards these events:**

- **The deaths and suffering caused by the war**
- **The decision to defend Berlin against the Russians**
- **The leadership of Hitler**
- **The destruction of Germany**
- **The end of Nazi rule**
- **The death of Hitler**
- **The way forward for Germany after defeat.**

2 **On your own, explain why Anna's and Erich's views about the fate and future of Germany are different.**

Postscript

Hitler told the German people he would make their 'one nation' bigger and stronger. But, in defeat, they have seen their nation divided by outsiders into two quite separate countries. You can learn about how and why this came about in Unit 7: Superpower Conflict. There you will discover that the German people had no control over their own destiny.

In some ways the destruction of Germany provided the people with a good chance to start again. Modern homes and factories soon sprang up. The West German people worked so hard to establish a strong and prosperous state that by the 1960s and 1970s their progress became called 'an economic miracle'. Shops bulged with goods and many citizens enjoyed a high standard of living. Nowadays, as Erich predicted, the West Germans are proud of their achievements.

But, as Anna predicted, the West German people have removed their blinkers and learnt lessons from their past. West Germany has been at the forefront of the new force of co-operation amongst the nations in Western Europe. This co-operation has resulted in organisations such as the European Economic Community (the Common Market).

Willi Brandt, who fled from Nazi rule, and later became Chancellor of West Germany, wrote in 1971 of a new spirit of *inter*nationalism (Source 24).

SOURCE 24

My years 'outside' had taught me to become a European. I became aware that this continent could not be rebuilt on the foundations of the old order of things: the nation state was a thing of the past.

The majority of my fellow countrymen have accepted my view that a nationalist cannot be a good German. The time has come for Germans to be at peace with themselves — so the world at large can become at peace with Germany.

1 **How do you think Erich would have felt about the separation of Germany into two countries in 1949?**

2 **What might Erich have thought of the progress made in West Germany since 1945?**

3 **What might Anna, now living in West Germany and in her 60s, think of her country's success at co-operating with other European countries?**

FALKLANDS WAR – MODERN NATIONALISM?

SOURCE 25 Victory celebrations in Argentina, 1982

Does your teacher remember the Falklands War in 1982? The Argentinians in Source 25 are celebrating the invasion of the Falkland Islands by the Argentinian troops. Argentinians believed that the British had no right to control the Falkland Islands. The islands, which they call the Malvinas, are only 400 km off the Argentinian coast, whereas Britain is more than 12,000 km away. When their troops invaded, the Argentinians celebrated for days.

ACTIVITY

Remembering the Falklands

Interview your teacher (or another adult). Note down the main point of what he or she says.
How did your interviewee react when:
a) the Argentinians invaded the Falklands
b) a British task-force set sail
c) British submarines and aircraft attacked Argentinian positions;
d) British ships were sunk
e) British troops forced the Argentinians to surrender
f) the Falklands became British territory again?
Study your interview notes. Try to decide what the overall attitude of your interviewee was to the British recapture of the Falkland Islands. Were they for or against the use of military force? Did they think a peaceful solution might have been found?
From this event, can you judge the *attitude towards nationalism* shown by the interviewee? Draw out a copy of this diagram:

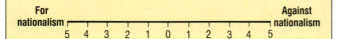

For nationalism 5 4 3 2 1 0 1 2 3 4 5 Against nationalism

Put a cross to show where your interviewee's attitude fits on this scale. Find out the views of ten other people and add their positions to your diagram. What do the results of your finished diagram seem to show?

Does your survey of Falklands attitudes show a wide range of views? Sending British troops to recapture the Falklands led to sharp differences of view. This is shown in the two Sources which follow.

SOURCE 26

OUR COUNTRY HAS WON a great victory and we are entitled to be proud. This nation had the resolution – to do what it knew was right.

WE FOUGHT TO SHOW that aggression does not pay. . . .

WE FOUGHT FOR OUR PEOPLE and for our territory.

WHEN WE STARTED OUT, there were the waverers and the fainthearts. The people who thought we could no longer do the great things which we once did . . . that Britain was no longer the nation that had built an Empire and ruled a quarter of the world. Well they were wrong. The lesson of the Falklands is that Britain has not changed.

THIS GENERATION CAN MATCH their fathers and grandfathers in ability, in courage, and in resolution. We have not changed.

WHEN THE DEMANDS OF WAR call us to arms – then we British are as we have always been – competent, courageous and resolute.

WE HAVE NOT LOST the ability. That is the Falklands Factor. We have proved ourselves to ourselves. It is a lesson we must not now forget.

. . . ONCE AGAIN, BRITAIN is not prepared to be pushed around.

WE HAVE CEASED to be a nation in retreat.

WE HAVE INSTEAD a new–found confidence. . . .

WE REJOICE THAT BRITAIN has rekindled that spirit which has fired her for generations past.

BRITAIN FOUND HERSELF AGAIN in the South Atlantic and will not look back from the victory she has won.

Putting the Falklands War in its place in history

Divide into groups of 5 or 6. Study Source 26 carefully. It comes from a speech made in 1982 by a politician.

1 Is the speaker a nationalist?

2 Try to decide who made the speech.

3 The speaker seems to be making four main points:

- Britain was right to fight
- Britain has not been getting weaker, whatever people say
- The Falklands War was like previous wars that Britain was involved in
- Britain will now be a stronger nation

Pick out the sentences which are used to support each point, and then discuss whether you agree with them.

The nationalism stirred by Britain's achievement in recapturing the Falklands was nicknamed 'the Falklands Factor'. It was a main reason why the Conservative government won a second term in office in Britain at the General Election in 1983.

Some people in Britain thought that the Falkland Islands, with their remote location from Britain, bleak climate and lack of resources, were not worth fighting for. This view is behind *Punch*'s 'joke-version' of the *TV Times* in Source 27. It hints that the nationalism stirred up over the Falklands was misplaced.

FALKLAND TV TIMES

SOURCE 27

9.00–9.01am: Good Morning Kelpers!
News, weather forecast, time check and What's on Today in the Falkland Islands

12.45 pm: Midday News,
if any; followed by **Recipe Time:** 40 interesting ways to fry seaweed.

1.30 pm: Teach yourself Spanish:
Emergency crash-course, day seven—how to say 'Please put that gun down and go away'.

5.00 pm: Playaway:
Making seaweed mats for Christmas.

5.10 pm: Interesting Places to Visit in the Falklands:
No 2, the post box.

6.00 pm: News, weather (rain)

6.02 pm: Sport:
Tonight's finals of the goldfish racing championships

10.15 pm: Closedown:
Live by satellite from England, Dame Flora Robson reads from the great war speeches of Margaret Thatcher.

Punch, April 1982 (adapted)

What points about the value of the Falklands Islands is Source 27 trying to make?

ASSESSMENT

Cause and consequence	1 The peace treaty of 1919 was designed to punish Germany for its part in the First World War. How far do you think the treaty can be blamed for causing the Second World War?
Empathy	2 Why did ordinary German people respond so enthusiastically to the ideas of Hitler and the Nazi Party?
Cause and consequence	3 What have been the main results of nationalism for Germany today?
Cause and consequence	4 This unit has looked at events in which national feelings have resulted in countries going to war with one another. Does nationalism always lead to war? Can you think of any examples from the past where nationalism has been a force for good?

5

DEMOCRACY

SOURCE 1 Unemployed people queuing for bread and soup, New York, 1930

THE USA WAS A very prosperous country in the 1920s. But in 1929 share prices collapsed on the New York Stock Exchange. Years of hardship and hunger followed (see Sources 1, 2 and 5). Between 1930 and 1933 the number of people out of work in the United States soared from 3 million to 15 million.

People lost confidence in the US government. It seemed either unable or unwilling to provide them with work and security. In October 1931 William Green, a moderate trade union leader, sounded a warning (Source 3).

SOURCE 2 A violent demonstration in New York, 1931

SOURCE 3

What shall we say of a system that relegates men at the prime of life to the human scrap heap? I warn the people who are exploiting the workers that they can only drive them so far before they will turn on them and destroy them. . . . Revolutions grow out of the depths of hunger.

Time, *October 1931*

Other countries were also feeling the effects of the crisis in the United States. In Germany unemployment had risen to 6 million by 1933. Many Germans were ready to turn to Adolf Hitler and his Nazi Party. He seemed to offer simple solutions to the problems and a strong leadership (see Unit 4: Nationalism). Would the United States follow the German example and abandon democratic government? F. D. Roosevelt, later to be President of the United States, spelt out the danger (Source 4). The US system of DEMOCRATIC GOVERNMENT was about to face a severe test.

SOURCE 4

People who are hungry and are out of a job are the stuff of which DICTATORSHIPS are made.

Divide into pairs and discuss this question:

Suppose you had been hoping to overthrow the American government and establish yourself as a dictator in the 1930s. What sort of promises would you have made the American people?

AIMS

In this unit we shall first be looking at what democracy is. We shall then be looking at some of the differences between democracy and dictatorship by making comparisons between the United States and Germany in the 1930s. You may discover that the differences are not always as clear-cut as you might expect.

You will also find out that not all change has to be violent. It does not always have to be brought about by revolution, war and terror. EVOLUTIONARY change is also possible — that is, change which occurs gradually — through debate, discussion and careful reform. Democracy can offer an alternative method of change — evolution rather than revolution.

SOURCE 5 A poor family in their shack in Tennessee, 1930s

WHAT IS DEMOCRACY?

The word 'democracy' comes from the Greek *demokratia*: *demos* meaning 'people' and *kratos* meaning 'rule'. So democracy means a form of government in which the people rule. But this still leaves many questions unanswered. Who are 'the people'? What is the meaning of 'rule'? Can all the people be personally involved in making decisions? Or should the people elect a group of rulers to govern for them?

Nearly every government in the world today claims to be democratic. Communist East Germany describes itself as an 'indivisible democratic republic' (Article 1 of the Constitution) in much the same way as West Germany describes itself as a 'democratic and social federal state' (Article 20 of the Constitution). Yet these two countries have very different styles of government. It seems that the word 'democracy' is now used to justify whatever rules, laws and policies a government makes. This was not always the case. Until the twentieth century democracy was not a very fashionable or popular form of government.

The world's first democracy was in Athens (Greece) in the 5th century BC. Thucydides (*c.*460–399BC) wrote about it (Source 6).

SOURCE 6

Our CONSTITUTION is called a democracy because power is in the hands not of a minority but of the whole people. When it is a question of settling private disputes everyone is equal before the law. . . . We Athenians, in our own persons, take our decisions on policy or submit them to proper discussions.

Thucydides, The Peloponnesian War, *fifth century BC*

What Source 6 does not make clear is that only 'citizens' could debate and vote. To be a citizen you had to be male and over the age of 18. Women, immigrants and slaves could not be citizens. As there were about 100,000 slaves and only about 40,000 citizens, Athenian democracy actually left out the majority of the people.

Athens: the world's first democracy was established here.

In Athens the citizens actually met in a huge open arena where they made decisions and passed laws themselves. This was only possible in small city states. With the development of large nation states a different type of democracy was needed. Citizens had to elect REPRESENTATIVES to make the decisions for them (see Source 7).

SOURCE 7

In a free country, every man . . . ought to be his own boss; the power to make laws should belong to the whole body of the people. But since this is impossible in large states, it is only right that the people should have representatives.

Baron de Montesquieu, *The Spirit of Laws*, **1748**

This type of democracy, where the people choose their representatives – their government – developed in Britain over several hundred years. It was a slow and relatively peaceful process.

Table 1 shows how Britain has advanced towards democracy over the last hundred years. Table 2 shows some of the main features of British democracy today.

TABLE 1
Advances towards democracy in Britain

1858	People no longer had to own property in order to stand for Parliament.
1872	Voting was to be carried out by secret ballot, so that nobody could know how somebody else had voted.
1884	The Parliamentary vote was given to all male householders over 21.
1885	The country was divided into 'electoral districts' so that all MPs represented roughly the same number of people.
1911	MPs were paid. Previously, only people with private money could afford to become MPs. Now the less well-off could stand for election too.
1928	The Parliamentary vote was given to all women as well as men.
1970	Young people could vote at 18 rather than 21.

TABLE 2
Main features of British democracy

1) All people over the age of 18 can vote, except lords, lunatics and criminals.

2) Elections are carried out by secret ballot. Anyone found guilty of bribery or corruption is severely punished.

A polling station

3) The country is divided into local CONSTITUENCIES, each of which sends one MP to a central Parliament.

4) People vote for candidates who represent different political parties. The party which wins the most constituencies (seats) usually forms the government, and its leader becomes Prime Minister.

5) The party with the second largest number of seats usually forms the Opposition Party, which normally puts the opposite point of view to the government.

6) A Parliament cannot last for more than five years. The voters then have an opportunity to elect a new government.

7) Before laws are passed they are debated in Parliament. A vote is then taken and the law is only passed if the majority of MPs have voted in favour. Laws also have to be passed by the House of Lords.

8) Everybody has to keep the laws passed by Parliament. However, people cannot be punished for speaking out against the government.

9) All political parties – and groups – are allowed to put their views freely in public.

British democracy has become the model for many other democratic states in the world.

The House of Commons

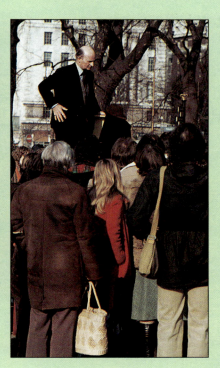

Speakers' Corner, Hyde Park, where anyone can address the public freely

DEMOCRACY OR DICTATORSHIP?

On 4th March 1933, Franklin Delano Roosevelt became President of the United States of America (see Source 8). He faced a grave crisis. This was the time of THE DEPRESSION. Farmers were having to sell their produce at very low prices. Industry was making half the number of goods it had done before the collapse of the Stock Exchange in 1929. Bands of homeless and unemployed people roamed the land. Roosevelt realised that to tackle these problems he had to increase the power of government. He had to show that democracy could cope with the problems. He had to prove it could provide strong leadership and bring about change without resorting to violence and dictatorship. If he failed to do this, then democracy in the USA might be swept away.

SOURCE 8 F. D. Roosevelt making his inauguration speech, 1933

Roosevelt wanted change without revolution (see Source 9). Previous American governments had done little more than maintain law and order. They had let businessmen get on with the important job of making money. Roosevelt was determined to make government into a sort of 'referee'. He wanted to make sure that ordinary people received fair treatment, even if this meant interfering with big business and being more 'directive'. He promised the American people a 'New Deal'.

Roosevelt shared many of the problems facing European dictators, like Hitler, but he tackled them in a different way. Some of his critics, however, accused him of using similar methods.

SOURCE 9 The evolution of the New Deal, 1934. This cartoon makes fun of Roosevelt's claim that his New Deal was evolution not revolution. The fruit on the tree carries the initials of the many new agencies he set up.

Talking to the people

Hitler was an excellent public speaker. Huge crowds of Germans came to hear him. He worked them up into a frenzy of excitement. He usually appealed to their worst instincts. In 1930, the *Observer* newspaper described Hitler's style of speech-making (Source 11).

SOURCE 11

Hitler is not a man but a megaphone. He has a surprising power of making patriotic noises and of shouting in perfect sincerity the most impossible nonsense against Parliaments and Jews. . . . He is dramatic, violent and shallow.

Observer, *September 1930*

SOURCE 10 A 1930s British cartoon making fun of Hitler's public speaking

Roosevelt also believed in talking directly to the people, but he preferred to use the radio. These talks over the radio were more like talks between friends than political speeches and became known as 'fireside chats'. They were calm, reassuring and informative. Frances Perkins described Roosevelt making these broadcasts to millions of Americans (Source 12).

SOURCE 13 A 1933 American cartoon, showing Roosevelt broadcasting to the nation

Tackling unemployment

SOURCE 14 Young Germans doing 6 months' compulsory service in the Labour Corps

When Hitler became German Chancellor in 1933 he promised 'work for all'. That meant creating 6 million new jobs. By 1936 he had found work for 5 million people and by 1939 Germany was actually short of labour. One of the ways he reduced unemployment was by forcing all male school leavers to spend 6 months in the Labour Corps. Here they did agricultural and forestry work. Hitler was quite clear about the kind of people he hoped would come out of the Labour Corps (Source 15).

Roosevelt also wanted to create jobs. He realised that it was the despair of hunger and poverty that drove many people to support dictatorships (see Source 17). Roosevelt was determined that Americans should not have to choose between freedom and food. He would prove that a democracy could support its citizens in hard times, and find them work, just as effectively as a dictatorship.

He set up a series of new agencies. The Civilian Conservation Corps (CCC), the Works Progress Administration (WPA), and the Public Works Administration (PWA) all provided men with jobs, ranging from agricultural work to the building of new schools, roads and dams. Even unemployed artists were found work, painting pictures on post office walls. Men were paid for this work and no one was forced to work against his will.

Desperate men were grateful for this opportunity to work and support their families. For many men the only alternative was crime and violence (see Source 18).

SOURCE 17

Democracy has disappeared in several other great nations, not because the people of those nations disliked democracy, but because they had grown tired of seeing unemployment and insecurity, of seeing their children hungry while they sat helpless in the face of government confusion and government weakness. Finally in desperation, they chose to sacrifice liberty in the hope of getting something to eat.

F. D. Roosevelt, a radio 'fireside chat', 1938

SOURCE 18

I hate to think what would have happened if this work hadn't come along. The last of my savings had run out. I'd sold or hocked [pawned] everything I could. And my kids were hungry. I stood in front of the window of the bake-shop down the street and I wondered how long it would be before I got desperate enough to pick up a rock and heave it through that window and grab some bread to take home.

Robert Sherwood, The Whitehouse Papers of Harry L. Hopkins, 1948

1 **What were the main differences between Hitler's Labour Corps and Roosevelt's work camps?**

2 **Compare Sources 14 and 16. What is the main impression given by each?**

3 **Hitler not only wanted to give young people jobs. He also wanted to change them (Source 15). In what way? Why?**

SOURCE 19 German workmen completing a stretch of autobahn (motorway)

SOURCE 20 A Field Office of the Works Progress Administration set up to direct the construction of a local road

Trade unions and worker participation

120,000 men were employed building motorways across Germany in the 1930s. Hitler admitted that the main purpose of these new roads was to transport troops and tanks in time of war. The workers had no say in deciding their hours, pay or conditions.

Trade unions were closed down and a Nazi-led 'Labour Front' was set up to control the workers and ensure peace in factories and workshops. Workers were not invited to take decisions or to help plan these projects. They were not made partners in government. The workers simply had to obey orders.

Men in the USA's labour camps were also told to build roads. But these roads were designed to meet community needs rather than military needs. American workers were not treated like slave labour. They were invited to help make decisions. They were also encouraged to join trade unions to safeguard their interests (see Unit 1, p.19). In 1935 the Wagner Act was passed giving every worker the right to join a trade union if he or she wanted to. Between 1933 and 1939 the membership of American trade unions rose from 3 million to over 9 million.

Roosevelt wanted individuals and communities to improve their lives. He wanted the people themselves to be involved at every stage of the process. He did not want to exploit people. The government would help and encourage people, not order them to do things.

Working people in the USA also had to overcome serious problems. These are described on pages 75–77.

SOURCE 22 A dam under construction in the Tennessee Valley

SOURCE 21

These fine changes we see have not come by compulsion [force] – for . . . thousands of townspeople have met together in the common effort. They have debated it and discussed it. Participating [joining] in the processes of their government – state government, local government, Federal government – they have altered the looks of their towns and their counties. They have added fertilizer to the soil. They have improved their industries. No farmer was forced to join this conservation movement. No workman was compelled [forced] to labor there . . . for less than a rightful wage. No citizen has lost a single one of these human liberties that we prize so highly in this democracy. This is a demonstration of what a democracy at work can do.

The best example of this community involvement was the Tennessee Valley Authority (TVA). The TVA was responsible for bringing back prosperity to the Tennessee Valley. It set up new irrigation projects, built dams and introduced new methods of farming.

In September 1940, when much of Europe was under FASCIST dictatorship, Roosevelt pointed to the TVA. He said it showed what democratic methods of government could achieve (Source 21).

1 Under Hitler how were workers treated? How did Roosevelt's attitude to the workers differ from Hitler's?

2 Examine Source 21 carefully. What does Roosevelt say is the great strength of democracy?

3 Explain in your own words how the government and organisations like the TVA behaved towards workers in the USA.

73

The lawcourts

When Hitler came to power in Germany he dismissed any magistrates and judges who were not Nazis. He set up a People's Court to deal with political (anti-Nazi) offenders. Very soon he controlled all the lawcourts.

Roosevelt did not try to do anything as drastic as this. But in 1937 he did try to reform the Supreme Court. The Supreme Court had the power to declare any law illegal if the law did not agree with the CONSTITUTION. The Supreme Court had used this power to VETO several of Roosevelt's reforms. Roosevelt decided to fill the Supreme Court with judges who supported him, so that this would not happen in the future. This alarmed Americans, who saw it as a threat to freedom and democracy. They did not want Roosevelt to interfere with the independence of their lawcourts. In the end Roosevelt's Bill to reform the Supreme Court was stopped by CONGRESS (Source 23).

> ### SOURCE 23
>
> We recommend the rejection of this Bill as a needless, futile and utterly dangerous abandonment of constitutional principle.
>
> *Report of the Committee of Congress,*
> *14 June 1937*

Roosevelt accepted this decision and never again tried to interfere with the lawcourts. He realised that in a democracy even a President cannot always get his own way.

> 1 Look at Source 24.
>   a What point was the cartoonist trying to make?
>
>   b Try to think of a caption for the cartoon.
>
>   c Do you think the cartoonist supported what Roosevelt was trying to do to the Supreme Court? Explain your answer.
>
> 2 What do you think was the most important difference between the way Roosevelt tackled the problems of the Depression and the way Hitler tackled them?
>
> 3 Hitler was, in fact, far more successful at reducing unemployment than Roosevelt. Does this mean that his methods were better? Explain your answer.

Democracy in the USA survived. Indeed, it was strengthened. Roosevelt showed that it was possible to overcome great problems and improve a nation's life without taking away people's freedom. He showed that democracy could bring about change. This change could be achieved peacefully with the agreement of the people. By 1940, Roosevelt felt optimistic about the future (Source 25).

> ### SOURCE 25
>
> All we have known of the glories of democracy – its freedom, its efficiency as a way of living, its ability to meet the aspirations [hopes] of the common man – all these are merely an introduction to the greater story of a more glorious future.
>
> We Americans of today – all of us – we are characters in the living book of democracy.
>
> *Roosevelt, quoted in J. Major,*
> *The New Deal, 1967*

SOURCE 24 Roosevelt lassoing the Supreme Court (*Punch* cartoon, 1937)

THE DARKER SIDE OF DEMOCRACY

Roosevelt spoke of 'the glories of democracy'. You might think that by saving American democracy he had saved a perfect system of government. This was not the case. Roosevelt's United States was a far fairer, freer and more open society than Hitler's Germany, but it still had its problems. Indeed, in parts of the United States things happened which were similar to those that were happening in Nazi Germany. There was a darker side to American democracy.

The Bosses

In some parts of the United States, mayors of cities and governors of states used their power to become virtual dictators. Huey Long, Governor of Louisiana, was one of them (Source 27). He had much the same sort of authority in his state as Hitler had in Nazi Germany. Harnett Kane described Long's hold over Louisiana (Source 26).

SOURCE 26

He possessed the state government, the university, all commissions and departments, the LEGISLATURE, the public schools, the treasury, the buildings and the Louisianans inside them. The courts were his . . . and he had the highest judges. He had a secret police which did everything he asked: kidnapped men, held them incommunicado [in isolation], inquired without check into private matters of opponents. He ran the elections. He counted the votes. He disqualified every man or woman he wanted disqualified.

H. Kane, *Louisiana Hayride*, 1941

SOURCE 27 Huey Long, 1930s

Attacks against minority groups

In the South and Mid-West of America the Ku Klux Klan (Source 29) terrorised and PERSECUTED Negroes, Catholics, Jews and foreigners. The people who belonged to the Klan were white American-born Protestants who were prepared to burn churches, beat people up and even lynch them in order to get their way (see Source 28).

SOURCE 28

The Ku Klux would whip men and women that weren't married and were living together. On the first day of January they would whip men and boys that didn't have a job. They kept the Negroes from voting. They put up notices: NO NIGGERS TO COME OUT TO THE POLLS TOMORROW.

B. A. Botkin, Lay Down My Burden, *1945*

SOURCE 29 Swearing-in new recruits to the KKK, 1930s

The RACIST beliefs and violent methods of the Ku Klux Klan were not so very different from those of Hitler's Nazi stormtroopers.

Organised crime

In most of America's towns and cities in the 1920s and 1930s, gangsters controlled everything from industry to trade unions. In Chicago, Alphonse Capone (Source 30) ran his own private army of thugs. He had more real power than the mayor elected by the people (see Source 31).

Gangsters like Capone took advantage of the weaknesses of democracy. They used these weaknesses to increase their own wealth and power. They controlled the police, lawcourts and trade unions in some cities, just as Hitler's Nazis did in Germany.

So democracy in the United States was not a perfect system. Beneath the surface there was crime, violence and unfairness. In fact, democracy is a very fragile system which it is quite easy to damage. After all, if you let people choose their own government then you run the risk that they may choose dishonest individuals. A clever politician can deceive, bribe or bully people into supporting him. He can use false promises and threats. Similarly, if you allow people plenty of freedom, there is a chance that they will use it badly, to commit crimes or to persecute other people. Democracy has to struggle all the time against these threats from within.

SOURCE 31

Already several unions . . . have been taken over completely by Alphonse (Scarface Al) Capone and his crew of gangsters. Other leading unions are being forced to pay monthly tribute ['protection' money] to stave off the gangsters. . . . With the unions under his domination, the gang boss would become a political power, able to swing many thousands of labor votes to servile candidates and officials [that is, to candidates and officials who would do as Capone said].

Chicago Tribune, *20 April 1930*

SOURCE 30 Al Capone, *Time* magazine, 1930

1 Huey Long was very popular with the poor people because he provided jobs and promised that if he became President he would guarantee every American family a home, a car and a radio. Do you think his 'dictatorship' was justified if he was using his power to help the weak in society? Explain your answer.

2 Why do you think the members of the Ku Klux Klan wanted to stop Negroes from voting in elections (Source 28)?

3 Is democracy a bad system of government because it cannot always control crime and violence? Discuss this question in a group and then report your group views back to the class.

Democracy today

All societies contain a wide range of different people with different interests, beliefs and ambitions. Democracy uses votes rather than bullets or force. It provides a way of changing society, steadily and peacefully, with the consent and support of the majority of the people.

But democratic government does not mean that all citizens have equal power, or that all people have the same influence over decisions. In a modern state it is just not possible for all people to be personally involved in their government. Instead, they usually elect representatives to govern for them. This means that some people are more active in political life than others and may also become more powerful.

Some governments today are obviously more democratic than others. But it is no longer possible to divide governments into the totally democratic and the totally undemocratic. As we have seen, American democracy in the 1930s included some very undemocratic features. Today, most governments around the world include some democratic ideas, but not very many are totally democratic.

ASSESSMENT

Empathy

1 Imagine you are a young American in the 1930s. Write a letter to your German pen-friend explaining why you think Roosevelt's methods for tackling the problems of unemployment and poverty are better than Hitler's.

Similarity and difference

2a Mixed up below are five 'principles of democracy' and five 'features of Fascist dictatorship'. Draw up two columns, one headed 'Fascist dictatorship' and the other 'democracy'. Write the correct entries under each heading.
   - Censorship of the television, newspapers and theatre. No freedom to say or write what you believe
   - Imprisonment of suspects or political opponents without trial
   - Government responsible to a Parliament elected by the people
   - Independent lawcourts not under the control of a political party
   - All adults entitled to vote (in secret) in elections
   - Only one political party allowed by law
   - Freedom to set up societies, clubs or trade unions and to organise meetings and demonstrations
   - Police force and armed forces controlled by laws passed by Parliament
   - No freedom to move around or to leave the country
   - Government rules by force and threats

 b Can you think of any other principles of democracy not included here? Look back to Tables 1 and 2 (pages 66 and 67).

Change

3 Terrorism (see Unit 10) attempts to bring about rapid change by using extreme force and violence. Democracy, on the other hand, prefers steady, peaceful change with the consent of the majority of the people. Make a list of the advantages and disadvantages of each method of bringing about change. Do you think it is better to bring about change by debate and persuasion or by force and threats? Explain your answer.

Investigation

4 Working with the rest of the class, produce a list of some of those countries in the world today which do not have democratic governments. Next to each country explain why it is not democratic.

6

CIVILIANS AT WAR

SOURCE 1

*W*HEN WARS BEGIN *people often cheer. The sadness comes later. The men from the town went off to fight. Rose and her mother joined the crowds and waved them goodbye. . . . Rose shivered with excitement. . . .*

Rose often went shopping for her mother. There were long queues outside the shops but no one grumbled. Everyone knew that food was needed for the soldiers. . . .

Many things didn't change at all. Rose still played with her friends and went to school early in the morning with her lunch in her satchel.

One day a lorry broke down. Suddenly a little boy leapt from the back of the lorry and ran

SOURCE 2

down the street. A soldier shouted 'Stop or I'll shoot!'

The boy ran straight into the arms of the fat Mayor. He dragged the boy back to the lorry . . . which he was thrown into. Rose saw other pale faces in the gloom. . . .

Rose was furious. Where were they taking him? She followed the lorry . . . through the town, across fields, under fences and barriers in places she wasn't meant to go. Rose took a short cut through the forest . . . then, in a clearing, she could hardly believe what she saw! . . .

Dozens of silent children stared at her from behind a barbed-wire fence. Their eyes were large and full of sorrow.

One called for food, others took up the cry. . . .

Rose told no one, not even her mother, what she had seen. All through the winter she took extra food . . . and headed towards the forest. The children were always waiting for her. When they took the food, through the electric wire, their thin hands trembled.

SOURCE 3

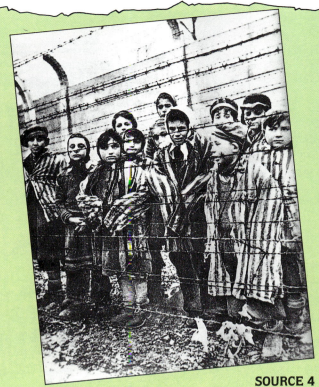

SOURCE 4

Even at night Rose made her journey. Others travelled under the cover of dark – soldiers, exhausted and wounded, poured through the town and on into the night. There was no singing or waving now. . . .

Then, one morning, the whole town decided to leave. People were frightened. They carried bags and loaded furniture on to wheelbarrows and carts. That was the day that Rose disappeared. Her mother searched frantically for her all over the emptying town. . . .

Thick fog shrouded the forest. It was hard to find the way. At last Rose arrived at her usual place. . . . Everything was so different. Behind her were figures moving about in the fog. . . . Tired and fearful soldiers saw danger everywhere. . . .

There was a shot. . . .

Rose Blanche's mother never found her little girl.

Adapted from Roberto Innocenti, Rose Blanche,
1985

SOURCE 5

This story of Rose Blanche is fictional. It was written by Roberto Innocenti in 1985. It describes the experiences of one little German girl during the Second World War (1939–1945). Experiences like these were shared by millions of other ordinary people who were caught up in the fighting.

Discuss and answer these questions in pairs:

1. List the ways in which this story can be used to discover details about civilians at war – queuing for food, for example.

2. The story is fiction but the photographs (Sources 2–5) are fact. Do they seem to support each other? Why do you think this is?

3. What value do you think the story has for the historian?

AIMS

This unit looks at the changes in warfare which have taken place in the twentieth century, and shows how they have affected civilians.

Through the centuries, soldiers have often inflicted suffering on villages and towns as they passed through. When Napoleon was attacking Russia in 1812, for example, the retreating Russian forces destroyed all crops, animals and supplies. They did not want to leave anything behind for Napoleon's forces. When this happened, civilians – ordinary people – suffered.

But before the twentieth century civilians rarely found themselves as the main target. All this changed with the First World War (1914–1918).

The written and visual sources in this unit have all been chosen to help you *empathise* with civilians at war. To help you experience and understand their feelings, many of the Sources involve young people.

THE FIRST WORLD WAR (1914–1918)

On 16th December 1914, shortly after the First World War started, Winifred Holtby, aged 16, was at school in Scarborough, Yorkshire (see Source 6).

SOURCE 6

I went down to breakfast and was raising my first spoonful of porridge to my mouth. . . . Crash! Th-u-d! The nerves in my system suddenly strung taut. The noise was deafening, clear-cut. I felt a tightness across my chest. . . .

Over the town hung heavy smoke, yellow, unreal. . . . I heard the roar of a gun . . . then Crash! and a thick cloud of black smoke enveloped a house in Seamer Road; a tiny spurt of red flame shot out.

The road was a stream of refugees – there was every kind of vehicle filled to overflowing with women and children . . . a young woman with a baby clutched in her arms; an old woman, only partly dressed, with her pitiful bundle of worldly goods in a rickety perambulator.

Just outside Seamer we sat down, tired out. As we sat, newcomers came with dreadful tales – 'the school was shattered' . . . 'the Grand Hotel was in flames' . . . 'the Germans had landed' . . . all this we took with salt.

Quoted in Vera Brittain, Testament of Youth, *1933*

REMEMBER SCARBOROUGH!

The Germans who brag of their "CULTURE" have shown what it is made of by murdering defenceless women and children at SCARBOROUGH.

But this only strengthens

GREAT BRITAIN'S resolve to crush the **GERMAN BARBARIANS**

ENLIST NOW!

SOURCE 7 Britain reacts to the shelling of Scarborough, 1914

Scarborough had just been shelled by German warships out in the North Sea. Over the following months they returned to attack other towns on the east coast of Britain.

Shortly after the first attack a new poster (Source 7) was issued by the British government.

Civilians were very shocked by the shelling. Now they felt themselves at risk, like the men in the trenches. But civilians were not only threatened from the sea. There was also a new danger from the air.

From January 1915 onwards, airships like the one in Source 8 bombed east coast towns and, a little later, London. Franz Lampel, a Zeppelin (German airship) navigator, described a raid on London (Source 9).

---

1 Study Source 6.
  a What do you understand by the word 'refugee'?
  b What evidence is there:
     i that the attack came as a complete surprise?
     ii that the civilians in Scarborough were badly frightened?
     iii that Winifred Holtby remained calm?

2 Look at Source 7.
  a What sort of language does the poster use? Pick out the words which you feel are particularly powerful.
  b What effect was this poster likely to have on British civilians?
  c How did the British government try to turn the German attack on Scarborough to their own advantage?

SOURCE 9

Over England at last! Below us the country is perfectly darkened. We must be right over London. The Commander stands ready on the bombing platform. 'Let go!' he cries . . . we hear the explosion . . . we have frightened them . . . a second bomb sets fire to something. On come the searchlights . . . like gigantic spiders' legs. We lose all track of time as we fly on, every half minute releasing another bomb.

Georg Neumann, *The German Air Force in the Great War*, **1921**

Reverend Clarke, an Essex clergyman, kept a diary of events between 1914 and 1919. He recorded people's fears of the Zeppelins (Source 10).

SOURCE 10

Thursday, 19th August 1915.
The baker's man told Mrs Everett that the Zeppelin was hovering, uncertain in its direction, over Great Waltham. A big motor which had been in waiting suddenly showed very bright headlights, and took the road to Chelmsford. The Zeppelin followed and when well on its way the motor put out its lights and disappeared.

Thursday, 14th October 1915.
Police Constable Cole said today that the report was that the Zeppelins were supposed to be making for Buckingham Palace.

[A later entry]
Leytonstone station has been laid flat, and forty-nine people killed. This news has been prohibited [kept back] because it is within six miles of London and it is not wished that the Germans should know how nearly they reached the capital.

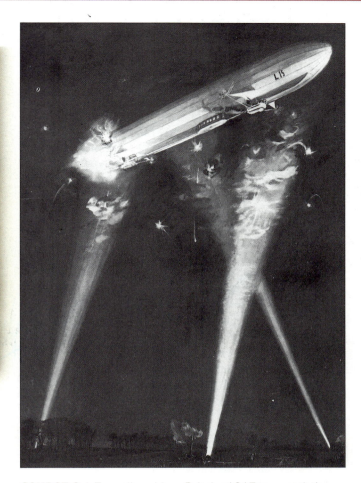

SOURCE 8 A Zeppelin raid on Britain, 1915 – an artist's view

1 What evidence is there in Source 9 that dropping bombs from Zeppelins was not very accurate?

2 According to Source 10, how did some Zeppelins find their way about the countryside?

3 Source 10 says that the British government CENSORED news during the First World War. Why did it do this? Do you think it was justified? Explain your answer.

About 1600 people were killed in Britain by airships or aircraft raids between 1915 and 1918. At the same time, British aircraft bombed parts of Germany.

The raids on Britain had a big effect on civilians. More of them were ready to enlist in the army. Their feelings towards the Germans hardened (see Source 11). Newspaper headlines called the Germans 'Hun baby-killers!'. People began to suspect that there were German spies in England guiding the bombers to their targets. Some people attacked foreigners who had German-sounding names or accents.

If you had been living during the First World War and your village had been bombed by a Zeppelin, would you have joined in attacks on foreigners? Explain your answer.

SOURCE 11 Anti-German feelings in Smithfield Market, London

THE SECOND WORLD WAR (1939–1945)

After the First World War military technology continued to develop. Weapons used during the First World War – like the submarine, the tank and the aircraft – were improved. Many more of these weapons were made and they were made much faster. They were produced in factories by MASS-PRODUCTION methods.

During the six years of the Second World War the United States produced 87,000 tanks, 296,000 aircraft (one every 5 minutes in 1943) and 315,000 artillery guns and mortars. All the guns could now fire further and faster. In the First World War, aircraft had mainly been used for reconnaissance. Now aircraft were designed which could fly longer distances so that they could drop more bombs over wider areas. On the eve of the Second World War, in 1939, Basil Liddell-Hart gave a warning of what this new technology could mean (Source 12).

The Spanish Civil War (1936–1939) had already shown what could happen. Spanish cities suffered heavy bombing – the first time this had ever occurred. Picasso painted a remarkable picture (Source 13) to show his horror at the bombing of one town – Guernica – in 1937.

> 1 **What message do you think Picasso is trying to get across in this painting?**
>
> 2 **Describe in one or two words how the painting makes you feel.**
>
> 3 **What can a historian learn from this painting?**

SOURCE 12

[Britain must] reckon with the possibility of an air offensive against London in which six hundred tons might be dropped in a day and continued for some time. . . . Nearly a quarter of a million casualties might be anticipated in the first week of a new war.

Gas attacks

Gas attacks were feared just as much as bomb attacks. The British and the Germans had both used poison gas in the trenches in the First World War. The Italians used gas bombs against the Abyssinians in 1935. It seemed likely that in any future war gas bombs would be used against civilians. The British government issued every household with a handbook on the effects of gas. It did not make very pleasant reading (see Source 14).

SOURCE 13 Picasso's 'Guernica' shows the horror of aerial bombing. It was painted in protest at the destruction of this small town in Spain by German bombers.

British civilians under fire

Britain suffered 60,000 civilian deaths in the Second World War. Most of these were through German bombing of British cities.

The first big German raid on London was on 7th September 1940. Over 1000 people were killed. Bombing continued every night except one for the next 76 nights. The raids were heaviest in the East End. Between September and November 1940, 200 tons of bombs fell on London every night. During the whole of the First World War only 30 tons of bombs had been dropped on London.

Later the Germans extended their bombing raids to other British cities. A 13-year-old girl described the bombing of her home in Liverpool in December 1940 (Source 15).

SOURCE 14

Ten minutes made it clear there was a lot to be learnt. . . . The effects of the different stuffs were varied and sensational. Phosgene filled your lungs with water and produced gangrene [rotting] of the extremities. Mustard had hardly any odour but blinded you and ate your flesh away.

Margery Allingham,
The Oaken Heart, 1941

---

1 How do you suppose ordinary people felt when they read details like those in Source 14?

2 If both sides had gas bombs, why do you think these bombs were not eventually used in the Second World War?

SOURCE 15

That night we were bombed out. After a dreadful night, with mobile anti-aircraft guns going off all around us and a tremendous number of bombs and incendiaries [fire bombs] falling, we heard different explosions which were later found to be 'land mines'. Soon after these, all resistance from anti-aircraft guns seemed to end and we could only hear bombs and the 'thud thud' drone of the German planes. Then they started dive bombing. It was bright moonlight and the first 'near miss' blew our windows in at the back of the house. The bomb didn't 'whine', it just sounded like a gust of wind before the explosion. My father dashed into the kitchen and could see the window blown out and the curtains in shreds. He shouted 'The blackout' and threw a kettle full of water on the dying embers in the grate! There were always 'lulls' in the raids, and during one of these, my father had a look out and saw that the whole area seemed to be on fire and there were lots of people shouting and firemen and wardens terribly active.

SOURCE 16 Three London children sit on the rubble that was once their home

---

1 Study Source 15.
  a What was the 'blackout'?
  b Why do you suppose civilians dreaded moonlit nights?

2 In two or three sentences, try to describe the feelings of one of the children in Source 16.

Evacuation

The British government tried to reduce the number of civilian casualties by EVACUATING children and young mothers from the big cities to 'safe' parts of the country (see Sources 17–20).

SOURCE 17

I was nine years old. . . . One night we went up to town to the theatre. Next day they labelled me, addressed me and packed me off to the country.

Derek Lambert

SOURCE 19

We were assembled in the playground, with our gas masks and our labels tied to our coats. Then we all moved away, with all the children and all the parents crying.

Bernard Kops

SOURCE 18 The journey begins — a group of evacuees, 1942

SOURCE 20 A teacher checks one evacuee's label, 1942

Some evacuees found that life away from home was not easy (Source 21). Many felt homesick, like Angela Stiff (Source 22).

SOURCE 21

Rose (my sister) whispered. She whispered for days. Everything was so clean. We were given face flannels and toothbrushes. We'd never cleaned our teeth until then. And hot water came from the tap. And there was a lavatory upstairs. And carpets. And something called an eiderdown. And clean sheets. This was all very odd. I didn't like it. It was scaring.

Bernard Kops, *The World is a Wedding*, 1973

SOURCE 22

At the top of the stairs was a chest of drawers and on top were the photographs of my family. So as I walked up the stairs each night I could see them. I felt very homesick and longed for letters from my mother. I used to kiss her photo 'goodnight' every night. My mother wrote regularly . . . but she only visited me once.

Angela Stiff, quoted in A. and A. Pike, The Home Front in Britain 1939–1945, *1985*

Angela Stiff and other evacuees also found returning home a problem (see Source 23).

SOURCE 23

When I returned to Croydon [from Yorkshire] . . . I met this lovely little girl . . . my sister, but she said, 'she's not your mummy, she's mine.' . . . I felt very rejected and left out. I had a Yorkshire accent, which was very different from everyone else's.

Angela Stiff

1 Look at Sources 17 to 23.
   a List the main hardships and problems faced by children who were evacuated from their homes.
   b What do you think you would have found most worrying and disturbing about being evacuated from your home?

2 Look at Source 23. What does Angela Stiff remember as the two main difficulties of adjusting to living at home again? Can you think of any other problems?

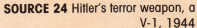

Arguing about evacuation

In 1944 the Germans started to use a new weapon called the V-1 (Source 24). This was a small plane with no pilot. It carried an explosive charge of one tonne. You could hear it chugging across the sky. When the engine cut out you knew you had only seconds to take cover. The first V-1 fell on London on 12 June 1944.

SOURCE 24 Hitler's terror weapon, a V-1, 1944

SOURCE 25 The effect of a V-1 attack, London

The best way to understand the problems facing London families with children is to put yourself in their position.

Divide into 'families' of six. Each family must then divide itself into three children and three adults – mother, grandmother and grandfather. Then role play a discussion about whether the children should be evacuated to relatives who live in North Wales.

The house opposite was recently destroyed by a V-1 (see Source 25). More attacks are expected at any moment. The neighbours have just evacuated their children because of these new air raids. Should the children in your family be evacuated or stay in London?

After you have finished the role play, each write up a brief report on how the argument went. This could include what was said, the part you played in the argument, how the adults and children reacted, and what was decided in the end.

The bombing of Germany

Of course, it was not just the British who suffered from air raids. Britain also bombed Germany (see Source 26).

SOURCE 28 Hamburg, after the bombing

SOURCE 27

. . . but before we even reach the shelter, a thunderstorm of noise explodes above us. It doesn't stop for even a second. The house shakes, the windows tremble. For two whole hours this ear-splitting terror goes on and all you can see is fire. . . . We sat with wet towels over our nose and mouth and the noise from one direct hit after another was such that the entire house shook and rattled, plaster spilling from the walls and glass splintering from the windows. Never have I felt the nearness of death so intensely. It is hard to imagine the panic and chaos.

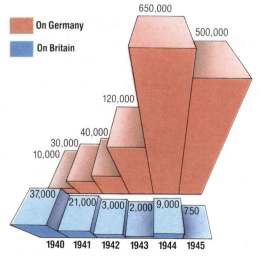

SOURCE 26 The volume of bombs (in tons) dropped on Britain and Germany

Source 27 is an account of an air-raid on Hamburg in July 1943. It comes from the diary of Mathilde Wolff-Monckeberg.

By 1945, Hamburg, like many other towns and cities across Europe, lay in ruins (Source 28).

By bombing German cities the British hoped to weaken German MORALE. They hoped the people would no longer want to continue the war. In recent years some historians have questioned whether this was a sensible idea.

a Do you think bombing civilians is likely to persuade them to surrender? Look back at Source 7.

b Can you think of any reasons why bombing might make civilians *more* determined to continue the war?

c Do you think bombing civilians in wartime is justified? Explain your answer.

Altogether Germany lost nearly 4 million civilians during the Second World War. Yugoslavia lost 1.3 million and the Soviet Union 7 million. Twenty-two million Chinese civilians were killed in the 8 years war with Japan. Some of these civilians died from disease and starvation. Some were murdered by enemy troops occupying their country. Others were killed by shelling and bombing.

THE ATOMIC BOMB 1945

Hiroshima and Nagasaki

In the summer of 1945 bitter fighting was still taking place in the Far East between Japanese and American forces. Casualties were very high. In the struggles for the islands of Iwo Jima and Okinawa 120,000 Japanese and 60,000 Americans were killed or injured.

Invading the Japanese mainland would cause the loss of thousands more lives. The US President, Harry Truman, decided to use a new weapon to bring the war to a fast end. The new weapon was the atomic bomb (see Source 29).

An atomic bomb was dropped on the Japanese city of Hiroshima on 6th August 1945 (see Source 30). About 78,000 civilians were killed instantly. Thousands died later from the terrible effects of RADIATION. A Japanese journalist described the scene (Source 31).

> **SOURCE 29**
> # 20,000 tons in a golf ball!
>
> One atomic bomb has a destructive force equal to that of 20,000 tons of TNT, or five 1000-plane raids. This terrific power is packed in a space of little more than golf ball size. Experts estimate that the bomb can destroy anything on the surface in a area of at least two square miles.
>
> *Daily Express*, August 1945

> **SOURCE 31**
>
> *Suddenly a glaring whitish pinkish light appeared in the sky. There was an unnatural tremor. This was followed almost immediately by a wave of suffocating heat and a wind which swept away everything in its path. Many were killed instantly, others lay writhing on the ground screaming in agony from the pain of their burns. Everything standing in the way of the blast – walls, houses, factories – was destroyed. The debris was spun round in a whirlwind and carried up into the air. Trams were picked up and tossed aside. . . . Trains were flung off the rails as though they were toys.*

> The Americans did not warn the Japanese how powerful the new bomb was.
> a Why did the Americans decide to drop the bomb on an ordinary city like Hiroshima?
> b Should they have given the Japanese some warning?
> c If you were an American soldier fighting the Japanese do you think you would have supported the bombing?
> d Do you yourself think the bombing was justified?

Three days later the Americans dropped a second atomic bomb, on Nagasaki. The Japanese finally surrendered.

The dropping of these bombs marked the end of an era. Any future world war was likely to be a NUCLEAR war. It would mean millions of civilian casualties.

SOURCE 30 The ruins of Hiroshima, August 1945

The future

Military technology has continued to develop since the Second World War. Computers are now used to steer aircraft, aim rockets and direct guns. All these weapons are faster, more accurate and more deadly than ever before.

More and more countries now have nuclear weapons. The superpowers (the United States and the Soviet Union) have enough nuclear bombs to destroy the whole world several times over.

There is also a new bomb, the neutron bomb. This can kill 120 times the number of people, while causing much less damage to property. It kills by radiation rather than heat and blast.

It is difficult – if not impossible – to defend against nuclear attack. In Britain, the Home Office has written a booklet called *Protect and Survive*. It suggests what to do to protect your family against nuclear attack (see Source 32).

Source 33 is from Raymond Briggs' cartoon book *When the Wind Blows*, which is about a man and a woman getting ready for a nuclear attack.

Many experts think that even concrete shelters would be useless. The heat from the blast would 'cook' the people in the shelters, even if they were 10 kilometres from the centre of the blast.

Some people believe that because a nuclear war would be so terrible it is unlikely to happen. They believe that nuclear weapons are a DETERRENT against war, that is, they actually prevent one from starting. Other people, like those who support CND (the Campaign for Nuclear Disarmament), feel that nuclear weapons cannot be justified on any grounds. They think that they should all be scrapped.

The Soviet Union and the United States often hold talks to try to reduce the number of nuclear weapons held by each side. At the moment there seems little possibility that they will agree to get rid of all of them altogether. The threat of a Third World War – a nuclear war – is still there. If this happened, civilians would suffer more than ever before.

Here are some ideas:

1. Make a 'lean-to' with sloping doors taken from rooms above or strong boards rested against an inner wall. Prevent them from slipping by fixing a length of wood along the floor. Build further protection of bags or boxes of earth or sand – or books, or even clothing – on the slope of your refuge, and anchor these also against slipping. Partly close the two open ends with boxes of earth or sand, or heavy furniture.

SOURCE 32 An extract from *Protect and Survive*

SOURCE 33 An extract from *When the Wind Blows*, 1982

1 What do you think is the point of developing a bomb, like the neutron bomb, that kills people but does not destroy too much property?

2 Look at Source 32. How safe does this shelter look? Why do you think the government produces booklets if there is no real defence against nuclear attack?

3 Look at Source 33. What point do you think Raymond Briggs is making about:
a how the man treats the official information;
b how the woman sees the situation?

ASSESSMENT

Comprehension

1 Look back at Source 7. Draw up your own poster, encouraging civilians to enlist.

Empathy

2 It is 1943. You are a thirteen-year-old who has just been evacuated from London after a wave of bombings in your neighbourhood. Write your diary entries for a week, starting with the bombings. Describe your feelings about the bombings and about being an evacuee.

Empathy

3 a Imagine you are a German civilian in Hamburg whose house has just been bombed. Write a short letter to a newspaper arguing against the bombing of civilians.
b Now imagine you are the pilot of a British bomber. Write a short letter to a newspaper explaining why you think it is necessary to bomb civilians in towns.

Change

4 About 1600 British people were killed by airship raids in the First World War. In the Second World War 60,000 civilians were killed. If there were a Third World War millions would be killed. List three or four of the main changes which have taken place in military technology since 1914.

Primary and secondary sources

5 Make a list of the different types of primary sources that have been used in this chapter. Do the same for the secondary sources.

Utility

6 Which Source do you think is the most effective at bringing home the full horror of modern warfare? Explain your answer.

To discuss

'For 35 years there has been peace in Europe – why? Because of the nuclear deterrent.' (*The Times*, 15 October 1981)

'I do not believe that the balance of terror has kept the peace over the last 30 years because I don't believe that there would have been a war without it. I believe the balance of terror increases rather than reduces the risk of war.' (M. Kaldor, *Why We Need Nuclear Disarmament*, 1981)

Discuss these two very different views in small groups. Then organise a class debate on the issue of nuclear weapons.

7

Superpower Conflict

BERLIN IS IN the middle of East Germany, which is a Communist country. The eastern half of the city – East Berlin – is the capital of East Germany. The western half of the city, however, is an outpost of capitalist West Germany, which is more than 150 km away to the west. This half – West Berlin – is like a capitalist island in the middle of a sea of Communism. The East Germans built the wall around West Berlin to stop their own people escaping to this 'island'.

Of course, this is not the first wall in history. You have probably heard of the Great Wall of China and of Hadrian's Wall in Britain. Both of these walls were built to protect rich empires against raids from neighbouring tribes. However, the Berlin Wall serves a very different purpose – this wall is designed to keep people in, not to keep them out. It is not directed against criminals, but against the ordinary citizens of East Germany.

What strange circumstances produced this isolation of half a city?

SOURCE 1

If straightened, the wall would measure 103 miles long. . . . There is more to the wall than this one structure. Behind it, one hundred yards into Communist territory, is another concrete barrier, almost as formidable. The levelled area between the two is a desolate, dangerous no-man's land, patrolled by Kalashnikov [Russian gun]-toting guards, dotted with free-fire machine-gun emplacements, and sown in places with landmines. It is punctuated by 285 elevated watchtowers, more suited to prison camps than city centres, and by a series of dog runs where ferocious, long-leashed Alsatians effectively run free. It is not a safe place to be. . . .

Floodlights and searchlights are positioned along the wall to illuminate it at night – an eerie sight. Specially reinforced obstructions have been erected at the handful of official border crossing points to discourage people . . . crashing through in vehicles.

Norman Gelb, *The Berlin Wall*, 1986

SOURCE 2 The Berlin Wall, from the west, 1980s

SOURCE 3

On the night of 23rd May 1977, Rainer Pekar and his friend, Uwe, attempted to escape across the wall from East Germany into West Berlin. Rainer was twenty-four and had already made two unsuccessful escape bids. He described what happened on this, his third attempt:

'Then we climbed over the first wall and scrambled over the electric fence in the death strip. Both of us had already reached the final wall when shots rang out. I felt impacts beside me and then I tumbled over into the West. Uwe had disappeared. I just heard him call out, "It's over, get going". I believe that he was hit.'

A. Kemp, *Escape from Berlin*, 1987

SOURCE 4 East German guards recover the body of a young man shot dead while trying to escape to the West.

AIMS

The world today is dominated by two superpowers – the United States of America (USA) and the Union of Soviet Socialist Republics (USSR). They both have the power to change and improve the lives of hundreds of millions of people. They also have the military power to destroy the world. The two nations have quite different deep-rooted beliefs and IDEOLOGIES. The government of the Soviet Union is Communist and believes in state control of all wealth and property. The United States is capitalist and believes that business and industry should be owned by individuals who can operate them for profit and can compete with each other. The great differences in the beliefs, organisation and government of these two nations mean that they have more often used their wealth and power to threaten each other than to co-operate to tackle the problems of the world.

This unit is mainly about this superpower conflict. It examines the origins of the struggle between the Soviet Union and the United States, focusing on their competing political ideologies as well as on their mutual fears and suspicions. It also shows, using Berlin as an example, how close to full-scale war the superpowers have come.

Above all, this unit tries to correct the misunderstanding that in any conflict someone must always be right and someone else wrong. In the superpower conflict both sides claim to be right. Different cultures, political systems and histories mean that they see the same events in very different ways. They have different perceptions of them. Each superpower is convinced that its rival represents the forces of evil and darkness. Only the shared fear of nuclear war and total destruction has persuaded these two nations to find some way of living together.

At the end of this unit you may conclude that, beneath the obvious differences, these two superpowers actually display certain similarities.

91

THE GROWTH OF THE SUPERPOWERS

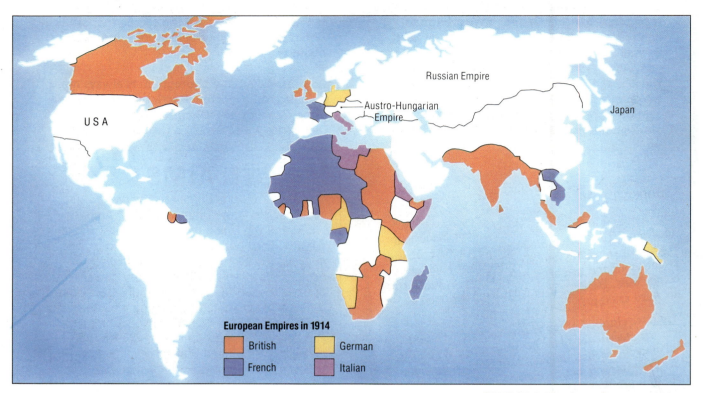

European Empires in 1914

- British
- French
- German
- Italian

SOURCE 5 The Great Powers in 1914

At the time of the First World War (1914–1918) there were no superpowers. Then there were eight 'Great Powers' – Great Britain, France, Germany, Italy, Russia, Austria–Hungary, the United States of America and Japan (Source 5). These Great Powers appeared to be of roughly equal strength and they settled the important world issues of the day among themselves.

By the end of the Second World War (1939–1945) this situation had changed. Austria–Hungary had been defeated and destroyed in the First World War; Germany, Italy and Japan had been defeated and weakened in the Second World War; France had been crushed by four years of Nazi occupation; and Great Britain, having fought against Germany for longer than any other country in the Second World War, was exhausted and almost bankrupt. On the other hand, the United States of America and the Soviet Union emerged from the Second World War much strengthened.

They were strong in different ways. The United States had developed huge industrial strength and had made the world's first atomic bomb. By 1945 she controlled a third of the world's industrial production and half the world's shipping. As the billboard (Source 6) shows, Americans were proud of their economic strength and prosperity.

By contrast, the Soviet Union had suffered terrible destruction at the hands of the Germans in the Second World War. Many of its cities and much of its farmland were in ruins by 1945. It was nowhere near as wealthy as the United States. But in order to defeat Nazi Germany the Soviet Union had developed massive military strength. By 1945 it had an army of six million men, 50,000 tanks, 20,000 aircraft and a growing navy. Source 7, showing Russian tanks at a victory parade in Moscow in 1945, illustrates the Russians' pride in their new military power.

1 **What does Source 6 tell you about 'the American Way'?**

2 **What sort of image of the Soviet Union does Source 7 suggest?**

3 **Look at the map of the world (Source 5). Why do you think the Soviet Union decided to keep her massive armed forces intact at the end of the Second World War while the United States did not?**

By 1945 the United States and the Soviet Union were so much stronger than the other nations of the world that they were called superpowers.

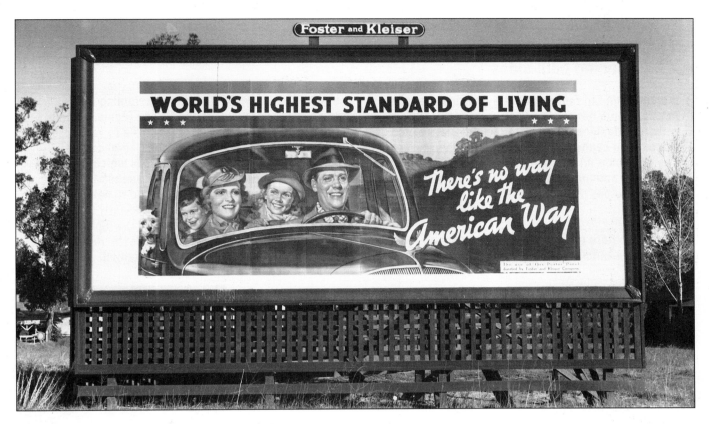

SOURCE 6 Billboard on a Californian highway, 1930s

SOURCE 7 Victory parade, Moscow, 9th May 1945

Origins of the superpower conflict

Although the United States and the Soviet Union had been allies in the Second World War, their friendship was unlikely to survive the coming of peace. This was because of the huge differences in the governments, economies and societies of the two nations. In 1917 a group of revolutionaries called the Bolsheviks had seized power in Russia and overthrown the Tsar (Emperor). After three years of bloody civil war the Bolsheviks established themselves in power. They then set about changing Russia into a Communist state. The old aristocracy was abolished and Christian churches closed. The nation's land, factories, shops and other businesses were taken over by the state which then controlled the entire economy. Only Communists had a say in the way the government was run. Anyone who objected might be arrested and thrown into prison.

This was very different from the way the United States was governed. The United States was a capitalist and democratic (see Unit 5) country. This meant that most land and most factories were owned by private citizens and that all adults had a say (through elections) in the way their country was governed. There was freedom of religious worship and no one could be imprisoned for their political beliefs.

Clearly, two such different systems of government would find it difficult to work together in peacetime.

ACTIVITY

Seeing both sides

It is important to realise that the Americans and the Russians both believe they are in the right. This activity is designed to help you to understand both sides of the conflict and to understand the reasons why each side mistrusts the other.

The two memorandums that follow are made up, but the Sources are real.

The Russian view

Pretend you are a Russian journalist working for *Pravda*, the official state newspaper. Your editor has instructed you to write an article explaining the origins of the conflict with the United States. To help, he has asked a Soviet historian to write to you, outlining the facts. The following memorandum is from the historian. It contains Sources which seem to indicate that the Americans are determined to destroy the Soviet Union and Communism and to dominate the world. Study the memorandum carefully and then write your article (of about 500 words) which is going to leave your Russian readers in no doubt about the USA's responsibility for the present conflict.

SOURCE 8

☀ UNIVERSITY OF MOSCOW ☀
MEMORANDUM

Memorandum on the US bid for world domination

Comrade,

We must never forget the twenty million Soviet citizens who died defending Mother Russia against Nazi invasion. Such a disaster must never be allowed to happen again. In future we must know our enemies and be prepared to resist them anywhere in the world. It is clear that the United States of America now poses the main threat to the Soviet Union. We must do all we can to warn our people of the American danger. The following information traces the history of America's campaign to destroy the Soviet Union. You may find it useful in writing your article.

1) The enclosed cartoon is a reminder that the United States and her allies, Britain and France, have already made one attempt to destroy the Soviet Union. [Source 8] During the Civil War (1918-1920) following the Bolshevik Revolution, the three Western powers sent armies into Russia to defeat Communism. The cartoon shows the rulers of the USA, Britain and France controlling the three savage Russian Generals who were leading the resistance to Communism.

2) Of course, the Soviet Union was forced into an alliance with the United States in the Great Patriotic War (Second World War) in order to defeat Nazi Germany. But the Russians never really trusted the Americans. The United States

SOURCE 9

deliberately delayed the invasion of German-occupied France (D-Day) until the Soviet army had already weakened and exhausted itself on the might of the German army. While Russians bled to death in the bitter struggle with Nazism, the Americans directed their puny military efforts to the remote areas of North Africa and Italy. It is now clear that the Americans wanted the German and Soviet armies to destroy each other so that the United States would be left free to dominate the whole of Europe. In July 1941 Harry S. Truman, later to become American President, said: 'If we see that Germany is winning the war we ought to help Russia, and if Russia is winning we ought to help Germany, and in that way let them kill as many as possible.' The Americans simply wanted to complete what the Nazis had begun - the complete destruction of Communism. The second cartoon shows the US army butchering our Communist neighbours in South East Asia. Are these American soldiers any better than the Nazis? [Source 9]

3) The final proof of American treachery is provided by the photograph of the explosion of the American atomic bomb on Nagasaki in Japan in 1945. This weapon has terrifying power, enough to destroy the world. This is too much power for just one country to be trusted with. Yet the United States refused to share the secret of this weapon with her Soviet ally. [Source 10]

The American President, Harry S. Truman, admitted this in 1945: 'The Joint Chiefs of Staff recommended that the United States retain all existing secrets with respect to the atomic weapons'. There can be only one possible reason for this secrecy - the United States hopes to use its nuclear weapons to bully and threaten the Soviet Union.

Who can seriously doubt the statement made by the Soviet Foreign Minister in January, 1949? [Source 11]

Now look at the last cartoon. It shows an armed, rich American soldier sticking flags in a map of Europe. The flags represent American military bases. Notice how they are surrounding and threatening Eastern Europe. In the soldier's back pocket an American politician waves an olive branch and shouts peace slogans. [Source 12]

The Soviet people must be warned of this menace before it is too late.

SOURCE 10

SOURCE 11

The Soviet Union is forced to consider the fact that the governments of the USA and Great Britain have adopted an openly aggressive political course, the final aim of which is to establish by force Anglo-American domination over the world.

ФРАЗЫ

МИР

ОБОРОНА

РАЗОРУЖЕНИЕ

И... БАЗЫ

SOURCE 12

The American view

Now pretend you are an American cartoonist working for the *Washington Post*. Your editor has asked you to draw a cartoon showing an aggressive Soviet Union threatening world peace. He has asked an American historian to send you a few details about the USA's past relations with the Soviet Union in the hope that they will provide you with inspiration for the cartoon. Read the following memorandum and then start drawing.

Washington University
MEMO

Memorandum on the Soviet bid for world domination

Dear Hank,

I hardly need to remind you that Communism is an evil force which aims to abolish all private property and to destroy all the rights and freedoms that America stands for. As the late President Truman warned in 1948, 'The USSR is a growing menace to the survival of freedom.' Consider the following points:

SOURCE 13

We consider it one of our main duties to give as much real help as possible to the workers' movement in other countries.

SOURCE 14

The Russians were coldly determined to exploit the helpless condition of Europe to further Communism rather than co-operate with the rest of the world.

1) The Russians have never tried to hide the fact that they intend to spread Communism through world revolution. This was clearly stated as early as March 1919, at the Comintern (Communist International) Congress. Look at what Zinoviev said. [Source 13]

2) The Soviet Union betrayed America's trust during the Second World War. The US Government thought it could rely on its Soviet ally and unselfishly sent the Russians all the supplies they asked for - everything from trucks to spam. And what happened after the war? The Russians showed their gratitude by betraying all the promises they had made at the Yalta and Potsdam Conferences. They turned the 'liberated' countries of Eastern Europe - Poland, Hungary, Czechoslovakia, Romania, Bulgaria and Yugoslavia - into puppet Communist states controlled from Moscow. President Truman complained of this in his memoirs. [Source 14]

The map clearly shows the scale of Soviet ambitions at the end of the Second World War. It proves that the Russians are not to be trusted. [Source 15]

President Truman voiced the fears of many Americans when he concluded, 'The Russians were planning world conquest'.

It is vital that the American public is warned of this growing Soviet menace before it is too late. The cartoon might give you a few ideas. It shows a greedy Russian bear, a red star on his cap, hungrily pawing the globe. [Source 16]

Can you produce something a little more striking than this. It seems to me Soviet cartoonists are getting their message across more effectively than we are.

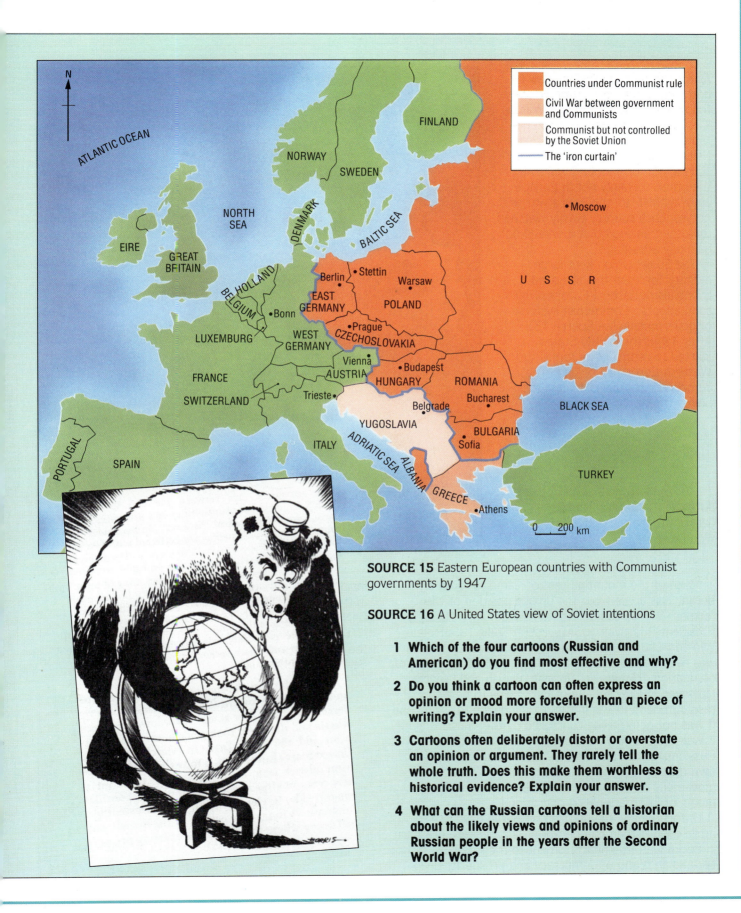

SOURCE 15 Eastern European countries with Communist governments by 1947

SOURCE 16 A United States view of Soviet intentions

1 Which of the four cartoons (Russian and American) do you find most effective and why?

2 Do you think a cartoon can often express an opinion or mood more forcefully than a piece of writing? Explain your answer.

3 Cartoons often deliberately distort or overstate an opinion or argument. They rarely tell the whole truth. Does this make them worthless as historical evidence? Explain your answer.

4 What can the Russian cartoons tell a historian about the likely views and opinions of ordinary Russian people in the years after the Second World War?

BERLIN – A BONE IN THE THROAT

As mistrust and suspicion grew on both sides in the years immediately following the Second World War, a 'Cold War' developed between the United States and the Soviet Union. Neither country was prepared to start a 'hot' or shooting war with the other, certainly not in Europe anyway. Instead, this was a war of nerves. Each country warily watched the other, anxious that it should not gain any advantage.

The Soviet Union kept large military forces in the 'liberated' countries of Eastern Europe, which soon adopted Communist systems of government (see Source 15). After 1948 the United States started to return large forces to Western Europe to defend 'free', democratic countries against the Soviet threat.

SOURCE 17 The Allied partition of Germany at the end of the Second World War

Much of the mounting tension came to focus on Berlin. This arose from the unique position of the former German capital. At Yalta, in January 1945, President Roosevelt (USA), Joseph Stalin (USSR) and Winston Churchill (GB) had agreed that when the war was over Germany would be divided into four zones of occupation – American, Russian, British and French. However, the capital city of Berlin was to be a special case. Although it was in the middle of the Russian zone it was not going to be controlled by the Russians alone. It was to be jointly controlled by the Americans, Russians, British and French. Each would have their own military garrison, but with rights of free movement throughout the city. Berlin was to be a model of international co-operation.

Unfortunately, the decision on Berlin gave rise to more conflict than co-operation. The Western presence in Berlin was an embarrassment to the Russians. It became an island of democracy and prosperity deep inside Communist East Germany. It also offered a 'hole' in the 'iron curtain' through which dissatisfied East Germans could escape to the West.

The Russian leader Nikita Khrushchev summed up the Soviet attitude in his various descriptions of West Berlin (see Source 18).

SOURCE 18

- a splinter that has to be removed
- a cancer that has to be carved out
- a bone stuck in the throat that has to be coughed up
- a rotten tooth that has to be extracted

The Berlin blockade

In June 1948 the Soviet Union cut all the road, rail and canal links between Berlin and West Germany. The map (Source 17) shows just how vulnerable West Berlin was to this kind of blockade. The Russian action was a clear attempt to force the Western garrisons out of the city to make way for a complete Communist takeover. The Americans and the British resisted this pressure by organising a massive airlift which kept the Western sectors of the city supplied with food and fuel.

A propaganda victory for the West

Not only was the Russian plan beaten but the United States turned this blockade to their advantage through clever PROPAGANDA. Propaganda is the art of spreading information designed to convert other people to your point of view. In a Cold War it is too risky to start using bombs and bullets, and so propaganda becomes the most effective weapon. The Americans were not slow to seize their opportunity. They portrayed the Soviet Union as a ruthless, heartless aggressor, starving innocent women and children. Photographs and films vividly presented the sufferings and hardships of the very young and the very old in the severe Berlin winter.

People around the world sympathised with the citizens of West Berlin. They came to see the American and British airmen as heroes and the Russians as villains. Sources 19 and 20 are just two of the many photographs which were published in newspapers around the world at that time.

SOURCE 19 Children watch the arrival of a United States transport plane, West Berlin, 1948

SOURCE 20 Berliners welcome the first lorry to arrive when the blockade was lifted.

The Berlin blockade convinced America and its European allies that the Soviet Union intended taking over the whole of Europe. To resist this they formed the North Atlantic Treaty Organisation (NATO) in August 1949. Source 21 shows the most important clause of the Treaty.

SOURCE 21

The parties agree that an armed attack against one or more of them in Europe or North America shall be considered an attack against them all.

Hardly surprisingly, the Soviet Union saw the formation of NATO as further proof that the Western powers were planning to destroy the USSR.

1 **What can these photographs (Sources 19 and 20) tell a historian about the Berlin blockade and airlift?**

2 **What other sources of evidence (apart from photographs) would your refer to if you were writing a book on the Berlin blockade?**

3 **If you had been a Russian photographer covering the Berlin blockade for Soviet newspapers, what sort of pictures would you have been looking for?**

4 **The existence of thousands of photographs of the Berlin blockade and airlift makes it easier for historians to study this period of history than, for example, the French Revolution for which there is no photographic evidence. Explain why you agree or disagree with this statement.**

The Great Escape

The blockade had failed but the Russians were determined to find some other way of forcing the Americans, British and French out of West Berlin. Their main worry was the huge number of East German citizens who continued to escape to the West through the city of Berlin. The West German government encouraged this exodus by accepting all East Germans as its own citizens. Between 1949 and 1961 one in every six East Germans abandoned East Germany for the West. They left at the rate of about 850 a day.

Those who left included: 16,000 engineers; 5000 doctors, dentists and veterinary surgeons; 1000 university lecturers and professors; 15,000 teachers; and 30,000 students. This mass migration was damaging East Germany's economy, and causing problems in everyday life (see Source 22). Khrushchev, the Soviet leader, later admitted how serious the situation had been (Source 23).

SOURCE 22

The entire workforce of a small rope-making factory went West en masse. People entered stores to find there was no one there to serve them. They went to offices to find that those with whom they had made appointments were no longer to be found. Plumbers, carpenters and other skilled workers were becoming vanishing species.

Norman Gelb, The Berlin Wall, *1986*

SOURCE 23

The drain of workers was creating a simply disastrous situation in the DDR [East Germany]. . . . If things had continued like this much longer, I don't know what would have happened.

Khrushchev, Khrushchev Remembers, *1971*

There were a variety of personal reasons why people left East Germany for the West. But there was also one very obvious reason which was clear to every visitor to Berlin in the 1950s. Sources 24 and 25 contrast the standards of living in the two halves of the city.

SOURCE 24

[West Berlin had] elegant shops flaunting the latest fashions and chic travel goods [and cafés where] the finest ice-cream sundaes . . . were to be had and . . . lush slabs of hazelnut *Torte* [cake] capped with outsized dollops of snowy, outrageously rich *Schlagsahne* [whipped cream].

Norman Gelb, The Berlin Wall, 1986

SOURCE 25

[In East Berlin] I walked past the open door of a greengrocer's shop and saw a queue of about twenty-five people. . . . I faithfully joined the queue to find . . . that I had been waiting for twenty minutes for . . . potatoes! . . . Meat is rather limited. . . . Butter at the moment is rationed to half a pound per head per week. . . . Often too in the summer months, butter and milk are 'off' before you have them home, as very few shops have refrigerators.

Mary Kellet-Long, quoted in Norman Gelb, The Berlin Wall, *1986*

1 Explain why the 'drain of workers was creating a simply disastrous situation in the DDR [East Germany].' How did it affect everyday life in East Germany?

2 What type of worker was a particularly serious loss and why?

3 Read Sources 24 and 25. Explain why so many East Germans wanted to move to the West.

The East German government tried everything to stop more people from leaving. People caught trying to escape to the West were sentenced to as much as fifteen years in jail. East German newspapers spread rumours that West Berlin was suffering from a serious polio epidemic. They also claimed that East German men lured to the West by 'slave traders' were forced into the West German army, while young women were forced to become prostitutes. None of these rumours worked. Clearly more drastic action was needed.

At a meeting with the American President, J. F. Kennedy, at Vienna in the spring of 1961, Khrushchev, the Soviet leader, threatened to treat Berlin like any other East German city and to force the Western troops out within six months. Kennedy feared that the Russians were planning another blockade of the city and that this time it might mean war. The last thing he expected was what actually happened.

The divided city

On the night of 13th August 1961, while the Americans were watching the routes from the West into Berlín, East German police and soldiers began building a barbed wire barrier to completely seal off the Western sector of the city from the Eastern sector and the rest of East Germany. Four days later work started on the building of a more permanent wall (see Sources 26 and 27). The Americans were completely taken by surprise.

1 Look at Source 26. Why do you suppose there are so many armed guards supervising the workers?

2 Look at Source 27. Imagine you are one of the West Germans in the group looking at the wall. Write down what you are thinking or what you are saying to the other people.

SOURCE 27 The Berlin Wall, from the west, 1961

SOURCE 26 Building the wall, 1961

Walter Ulbricht, the East German President, claimed that the wall was necessary to keep undesirable people from the West out of his country. He listed the kinds of people he didn't want (Source 28).

The West saw a much more sinister purpose behind the building of the wall – to imprison the citizens of East Germany (see Source 29).

> Sources 28 and 29 offer very different interpretations of the reasons for building the Berlin Wall. Which do you think is the more reliable? Explain your answer.

SOURCE 28

. . . counter-revolutionary filth, spies and diversionists, speculators and traffickers in human beings, prostitutes and corrupted teddy boys . . .

Pravda, *28th August 1961*

SOURCE 29 Ulbricht is declaring: 'All the DDR is now forbidden territory. The whole population has been evacuated to China. I announce the existence of total state security.'

Although the Soviet Union had broken the four-power agreement by building a wall across the centre of Berlin, the United States was not prepared to fight a war over this issue. Once they had recovered from their surprise, the Americans contented themselves with a few token acts of defiance, such as increasing their garrison in Berlin and, on one occasion, driving their tanks right up to one of the crossing points in a show of strength (Source 30).

The wall certainly stopped the flood of East German refugees to the West, and in time strengthened the DDR. But, as you saw at the beginning of the unit, isolated escape attempts have continued.

SOURCE 30 United States and East German tanks confront each other, Berlin, 1961

Superpower flashpoints

At the moment Berlin is no longer a FLASHPOINT, but the superpowers are still competing and clashing in other parts of the world. Of course, Berlin was especially dangerous because the USA and the Soviet Union were face to face. In other parts of the world the superpowers have tried to avoid this sort of head-on confrontation. By and large they have accepted that they each have 'areas of influence and control' and that they will not threaten each other's vital interests.

For example, in 1962 Khrushchev finally withdrew Soviet missiles from Cuba because he realised that the USA felt strongly enough about this issue to fight a war over it. Similarly, the USA made no serious attempts to interfere when the Soviet Union invaded Hungary in 1956 and Czechoslovakia in 1968. The superpowers have enough respect for each other's military strength to act cautiously. They also realise that a careless move or an accident could trigger a war between them.

This fear has resulted in several meetings between the superpowers to try to control or reduce the number of nuclear weapons they each possess. From 1969 onwards relations between the two superpowers did improve dramatically. This period of 'détente' (a relaxation of tension) lasted for about ten years, but any long-term agreement between them was made impossible by their wide differences of outlook. The United States remained determined to check the spread of world Communism, using force where necessary. It invaded Grenada in 1983 and started sending financial and military aid to the anti-Communist forces in Nicaragua in 1984. The Soviet Union was equally determined to defend its interests and as a result invaded Afghanistan in 1979.

Mikhail Gorbachev's appointment as the leader of the Soviet Union in 1985 introduced a new chapter in Soviet-American relations. In 1987 both superpowers agreed to reduce their nuclear arsenals and the following year Gorbachev started the withdrawal of Soviet troops from Afghanistan.

In an address to the United Nations in December 1988, Gorbachev proposed a whole new philosophy of international relations, based on interdependence, co-operation and listening to other nations. He backed this 'new thinking' with plans to cut Soviet forces in eastern Europe by 500,000 men, 10,000 tanks and 800 planes. For once there was more talk of co-operation than conflict.

ASSESSMENT

Similarity and difference

1 At the start of this unit you were asked to be on the look-out for similarities and differences between the United States and the Soviet Union. In what way do you think these two superpowers are most alike? In what way are they most different?

Inference

2 Read Sources 24 and 25. Would it be fair to infer from just these two Sources that capitalism (Source 24) is always a more successful system than Communism (Source 25)? Discuss your ideas with the rest of the class.

Comprehension

3 This unit includes three maps. Why is a knowledge of world geography useful to an understanding of the superpower conflict?

Investigation

1 The United States and the Soviet Union are almost certainly arguing over some part of the world at this very moment. Using newspapers and magazines, compile a 'Superpower conflict' scrapbook. This should include pictures and newspaper cuttings as well as your own comments and observations. You could do this as a class project.

2 Try to find out about life in the Soviet Union today. Look at such things as education, housing, entertainment, the press and employment. In what ways does life in the Soviet Union differ from life in Western Europe? Do you think life in the West is better? Why?

8

COLONIALISM to INDEPENDENCE

ON 21ST MAY 1930, 2500 Indians gathered outside the wired-off government salt depot in Dharasana. They were not carrying any weapons. Facing them were 400 Indian policemen commanded by six British officers. They carried long clubs with steel tips. The Indian leader, Mrs Sarojini Naidu, spoke to the Indians: 'You will be beaten but you must not resist. You must not even raise a hand to ward off blows.'

In total silence, one group at a time, the Indians approached the depot. They did not fight back as they were beaten senseless by the police. Onlookers were horrified. Among them was Webb Miller, an American journalist, who reported on the scene (Source 2).

SOURCE 2

Those struck down fell sprawling, unconscious or writhing in pain with fractured skulls or broken shoulders. In two or three minutes the ground was quilted with bodies. Great patches of blood widened on their white clothes.

Then another column formed. Although every one knew that within a few minutes he would be beaten down, perhaps killed, I could detect no signs of wavering or fear. There was no fight, no struggle; the marchers simply walked forward until struck down.

In a temporary hospital set up by the police, Miller counted 320 injured Indians who had been taken prisoner. Many were unconscious. Two were already dead. Miller's damning report of the event appeared in newspapers around the world.

The most revealing comments on the incident came from Indian and British politicians. V. J. Patel, an Indian NATIONALIST leader present at Dharasana, saw the incident as the last straw (Source 3).

SOURCE 1 A scene from the film *Gandhi* showing the protesters approaching the police outside the salt depot at Dharasana

SOURCE 5 An 1886 map of the British Empire

SOURCE 3

All hope of reconciling India [making India friendly] with the British Empire is lost forever. I cannot understand how any government that calls itself civilised could deal as savagely and brutally with non-violent, unresisting men as the British have this morning.

But Lord Irwin, the VICEROY who administered India for Britain, made light of it when he wrote to King George V (Source 4).

SOURCE 4

Your Majesty can hardly fail to have read with amusement the accounts of the several battles for the salt depot.

To understand the events at Dharasana you need to be able to untangle several threads of the story of the British in India. You will do this as you work through this unit. For the time being, it is enough to think about what you have read here.

> **Divide into pairs. Is there anything which puzzles you about the events? For example, why did Indian policemen club other Indians? Why was there so much fuss about a salt depot? Write down all the questions you feel are raised by the events described. Share them in a class discussion.**

AIMS

In this unit we shall be looking at British rule in India as one example of COLONIALISM. We shall study the process of colonisation by examining the *causes* of it — from Britain's point of view — and the *effects* of it — from the colony's point of view.

In setting up and maintaining a vast overseas empire (see Source 5), Britain was typical of many European countries between 1600 and 1945. The whole issue of colonialism is one which has generated much debate in history; you will be asked to judge different opinions of it.

The second part of this unit looks at how India achieved INDEPENDENCE from Britain. It focuses on the role of one important individual, Mahatma Gandhi, and explores how he contributed to the growth of Indian nationalism.

India's struggle for independence from the British Empire is one example of a worldwide trend from colonialism to independence after 1945. The last part of this unit looks at how Africa gained independence from the many European countries who colonised it. It also examines whether some of the problems now facing the independent states have their roots in Africa's colonial past.

HOW DID THE BRITISH COLONISE INDIA?

India developed an advanced civilisation from about 2000 BC onwards. Cities, palaces and temples were built. Fine cloth was produced. In the 1600s and 1700s India was at the centre of a vast network of world trade, exporting goods to West Africa, the Far East and Europe. European colonists, first from Portugal and later from France and Britain, began to compete for wealth within this subcontinent.

From 1600 to 1857 British interests in India were looked after by the British East India Company. This was originally founded as a trading company of merchants, with headquarters in London.

At first the East India Company concentrated on establishing a series of trading centres, called 'factories', such as the one at Surat shown in Source 6. Here Indian goods were collected for export to Britain, and imports from Britain could be sold. As the power of the Company grew it extended its interests. In addition to trade, it became involved in military defence and political control, expanding its activities on Britain's behalf.

Source 7 shows the increasing extent of Indian territory either under direct British rule (shaded pink) — or under the control of local princes (shaded yellow). The princes administered the land for Britain in a way similar to the medieval system of feudalism which you learned about in Book 1.

After an unsuccessful uprising by Indian soldiers in the British army in 1857, control of India passed from the East India Company directly to the British government. India was administered by a Viceroy assisted by relatively small numbers of the army and Civil Service.

SOURCE 6 A British East Indian Company trading base at Surat, early seventeenth century

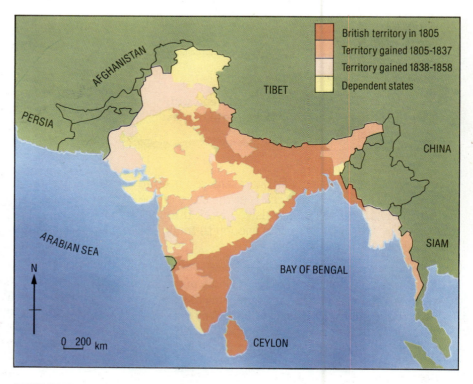

SOURCE 7 Nineteenth-century India: Britain's increasing control

Colonialism and cotton

You have already seen in Unit 1 how, during the Industrial Revolution, Britain increased its output of textiles using new machinery in factories. It then needed bigger markets to sell goods in. Since Britain's population of 15 million could only buy so much, the colonies were the obvious choice to sell to.

But there was a problem with India. India already exported 13 times more cloth to Britain than it imported from Britain. By 1815 the trade between India and Britain for finished cotton cloth looked like this:

Indian exports to Britain

British exports to India

1815

ACTIVITY

What could the British government do to reduce Indian exports?

1 In small groups consider these possible courses of action:
   A **Do nothing** – trade and production could continue without government interference.
   B **Place a tax on the cotton produced in India** – this would make Indian cotton more expensive to produce, and more expensive for Britain to import – so less would be bought.
   C **Place import controls in Britain on Indian cloth** – this would reduce the amount of imports to Britain and restrict Indian exports.
   D **Ban production of cotton in India.** The government could order, and the army enforce, the closure of all cotton mills in India.

2 Discuss and decide which of these policies might be:
   ● the most effective
   ● the least effective
   ● the easiest to operate
   ● the most difficult to operate

3 Which of these policies would do most to encourage exports of British cotton to India?

What did happen?

By 1813 cotton goods from India carried import duties of 85%. The East India Company taxed Indian cloth production at up to 55% of its value. The effects are shown below.

Indian exports to Britain

British exports to India

1832

British cotton exports to India rose 16 times! Indian exports fell by more than 90%!

It became cheaper for Indians to send raw cotton to Britain to be made into cloth than to produce it themselves. The result was the collapse of the Indian textile industry. In Madras the incomes of weavers fell by 75% between 1813 and 1844, causing widespread hardship. In 1840, Governor-General Bentinck talked of 'the bones of the cotton weavers bleaching the plains of India'.

Many weavers, and other craftsmen, were forced back on to the land (see Source 8), having to live off smaller plots.

SOURCE 8

The population of Dacca has fallen from 150,000 to 30,000 . . . jungle and malaria are fast encroaching. Dacca, which was the Manchester of India, has fallen off from being a very flourishing town to a very poor and small one . . . the distress there has been very great indeed.

Sir Charles Trevelyan, 1840

Indians now bought Lancashire cotton. In this way the Lancashire men and women got jobs, British cotton merchants and shippers got the profits, and the Indians went out of business. Britain got richer. India got poorer.

The enforced decline of the Indian cloth industry is important. It reflects one of the worst features of colonialism. It also, as you will see later, played a key role in the story of how India struggled for independence from Britain. Mahatma Gandhi made cotton production a main issue in his life-long campaigns – he saw it as a symbol of India's enforced submission to Britain.

THE RAJ: RULERS AND RULED

The period of British control of India up to 1947 was known as the Raj (rule). The Sources in this section try to create an image of what it might have been like to live in India from the point of view of the ruling British and the ruled Indians.

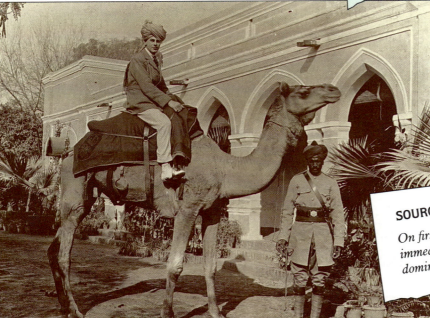

SOURCE 9 Camel transport, 1912

SOURCE 14 A tiger hunt, Mysore, 1892

SOURCE 15 A social gathering, 1890s

SOURCE 16 Tiffin by the roadside, Bhujji State, 1912

SOURCE 17

Once the style of the Raj had been struck by 1877 very little changed.

Charles Allen, historian, 1977

SOURCE 19 The British rulers, as seen by an 1800s Indian painter

SOURCE 18

I hate the British for the wrong that they have done in India. Their Parliament makes laws for us and their government appoints a Viceroy to rule over us. The British are arrogant, despising our brown skins. Worst of all the British have kept us poor. Our people toil for slave wages in British cotton mills and on British tea plantations.

Pandit Nehru, India's first Prime Minister after Independence

Do the photographs strengthen or weaken the image of British rule given in the written sources?

ACTIVITY

The colonialism debate

In groups, read carefully through the material which follows. It gives the two sides to the colonialism debate, using a number of written and visual sources. Once you have read through the material, answer the questions which follow, and then report back your group's view on each question in a class discussion.

The pro-Empire view

Views about colonialism in general, and the British Empire in particular, have changed considerably this century. Up to the Second World War (1939–1945) British history books, and many history lessons, were strongly in support of the British Empire. So many generations of children were taught the 'benefits' of Empire, as outlined in Source 20.

SOURCE 21 *Punch* cartoon, April 1894

A 19th century cartoon (Source 21) is an example of the popular image of Britain's kindliness to the 'less fortunate' of the world.

It is not only past generations and primary sources which reflect the pro-Empire view. In a recent book about the British in India, Philip Mason puts forward a similar view (Source 22).

SOURCE 20

Law and Order is perhaps the most important advantage that we British gave to our colonies. People could go about their daily duties without fear of attack by others.

We took the ideas of liberty, equality, justice and democracy to the colonies. With these came the advantage of civilisation closely followed by the benefits of technology.

What were these advantages? First – ease of travel, secondly – education, thirdly – public health. In addition to the fight against disease, our experts helped to provide sanitation and pure water supplies.

Also, there were improvements in agriculture. The products of this could be sold at a profit to all concerned.

A British Colonial Administrator

SOURCE 22

There comes a time in a man's life when he may well stand back and consider what he has done and whether it was worth doing. If in such a mood, the English look back on their varied history, the long connection with India will be an achievement that cannot be ignored.

The heart will beat faster . . . to remember how a handful of his countrymen mastered and ruled so many millions . . . . the main matter of pride will be that so few amongst so many had so slight a need for force.

Philip Mason, *The Men Who Ruled India*, 1985

The anti-Empire view

In recent years an 'anti-Empire' view has arisen. In its mildest form, this view proposes that the British may have harmed India, though not on purpose (see Source 23).

SOURCE 23

The Raj brought with it foreign people who were, in their own curious way, wary of India and yet loved it. Not always in the right way, perhaps, and not always doing what was best for India. . . . By and large they meant well.

Charles Allen, *A Scrapbook of British India*, 1977

A more extreme anti-Empire view claims that colonialism was RACIST. Those who support this view say that the white people of the colonial power felt themselves to be naturally superior to the non-white people they governed. They therefore treated them as inferiors, kept them from any form of power, and EXPLOITED them as a workforce (see Source 24).

SOURCE 24

Racist social systems were developed wherever countries were brought under colonialism. . . . Such systems ensured that the local people provided cheap labour and had no rights over any wealth they produced, little of which was used for their benefit

Institute of Race Relations, Patterns of Racism, *1982*

In line with this view, primary sources such as the photograph in Source 25 can be seen as examples of the 'evils' of Empire and colonialism.

In groups discuss these questions. Take notes so that you can compare your answers in a class discussion.

1 Look back to Source 20. It claims 'benefits' for the colony in being part of the British Empire. Which of the benefits were based on Britain's
   a motive of making trading profits?
   b care for the welfare of the native people?
   c racist beliefs in European people's superiority over non-white peoples?

2 Which of the above three views does Source 21 most closely link to? Discuss in detail what the cartoon is trying to say. How effective is it?

3 Philip Mason, who wrote the extract in Source 22, had been a member of the Indian Civil Service in the 1920s and 1930s. Does that make his view:
   a trustworthy, because he lived and worked in India for 20 years?
   b untrustworthy, because he wrote down his views more than 40 years afterwards?
   c useless to an historian because of his 'pro-Empire' attitude?

4 Source 24 is taken from a book produced by the Institute of Race Relations. It, like Source 22, is a secondary source. Do you think it is likely to be more trustworthy or less trustworthy than Source 22? Why?

SOURCE 25 Indian cotton awaits export to Britain, 1880s

INDIAN INDEPENDENCE – THE CRUSADE OF MAHATMA GANDHI

Unlike many of the great figures of the 20th century, Mahatma Gandhi never held high office. Yet his power to control the actions of millions was immense. He believed passionately in the injustice of British colonial rule in India. But he believed equally firmly that Indian independence had to be gained by non-violent means.

Gandhi said of violence: 'I object to violence because when it appears to do good, the good is only temporary: the evil is permanent.' He believed that truth and right would always win in the end.

Gandhi's 20s and 30s were spent working as a barrister in South Africa, where he fought 'non-violently' against racial prejudice. At 45, he returned to India. Believing that Britain's power over India was symbolised by the huge imports of British cloth, he refused to wear bought clothing. He spent part of every day spinning (Source 26) and wove simple cloth called *khadi*. Both the *khadi* and the spinning wheel became, to Gandhi's followers, symbols of Indian self-sufficiency and independence. The spinning wheel was later used in the design of the Indian flag (Source 27).

Actions and reactions 1919–1948

The rest of this section will consider key events in India's progress to independence. For each event, we look at what Gandhi did, and at how Britain reacted to what he did.

SOURCE 27 India's flag

SOURCE 26 Gandhi spinning in Calcutta, 1925

EVENT: FIRST WORLD WAR 1914–1918

The First World War saw hundreds of thousands of Indians fight for Britain (Source 28). In return for this service Indians hoped for a greater say in running their own affairs. This was not to be. Britain actually increased the restrictions in 1919.

FROM INDIA — SIKHS ON THE MARCH IN FRANCE

SOURCE 28 Indian troops on the Western Front, from the *Graphic*, December 1914

GANDHI'S ACTION: 1919 HARTAL

Gandhi felt betrayed by Britain's action. He called a general strike — a *hartal* — throughout India for one day. On the day, 300 million people brought India to a standstill by praying and fasting. Against Gandhi's wishes, violence broke out in some areas.

BRITISH REACTION: 1919 AMRITSAR MASSACRE

British fears of a general revolt in the Punjab led to arrests of Indian politicians in Amritsar, one of the main cities in northern India. Indians protested and the authorities called for army reinforcements, led by General Dyer. Dyer ordered his men to open fire on a large crowd of unarmed Indians attending a meeting in the city. No warning was given, and 10 minutes continuous fire left 379 dead and 1200 wounded. Dyer explained his actions (Source 29).

SOURCE 29

My idea . . . was to make a wide impression throughout the Punjab. It was a merciful act, though a horrible act, and they ought to be thankful to me for doing it.

SOURCE 30

The British Government today represents satanism. When a government takes up arms against its unarmed subjects then it has forfeited the right to govern.

Gandhi, 1919, quoted in R. W. Rawding, Gandhi, 1980

Following the massacre, Dyer set up a series of punishments for the Indians. These included the 'Crawling Order', whereby Indians wishing to use a particular street in Amritsar were forced to crawl on their hands and knees as a mark of respect to the British.

The events of Amritsar convinced Gandhi that the British presence in India had become an evil (Source 30).

The Amritsar Massacre was a turning point. After it, Gandhi became the leader of the Indian nationalists in the Indian Congress Party. He resolved to work towards Indian independence by a series of major campaigns against the British.

GANDHI'S ACTION: 1920 'NON-CO-OPERATION'

Gandhi's first campaign was based on 'non-co-operation'. It took many forms. He called for British imported goods, especially cloth, to be boycotted. British schools, courts and offices were also to be boycotted. Peasants were to refuse to pay their taxes.

For months Gandhi toured the country, explaining the purpose of his ideas, which he claimed would bring home rule within 12 months. Everywhere he went he encouraged supporters to burn foreign clothing and to spin and weave each day.

In 1921 the nationalist Congress Party agreed to Gandhi's request for a national non-violent campaign of civil disobedience.

But, in spite of Gandhi's wishes, violence broke out in several places. Gandhi was appalled. He went on a five-day fast and called off the campaign. India, he concluded, was not yet ready for independence through non-violent action.

BRITISH REACTION: 1922

At the start, the British dismissed the non-co-operation movement. As time passed they realised the threat that Gandhi posed. In March 1922 Gandhi was arrested and charged with sedition (encouraging others to disobey the law).

The case against Gandhi was clear cut. He himself had written about non-co-operation and the law (Source 31).

Gandhi pleaded guilty. The trial gave Gandhi the opportunity to publicise his views (Source 32).

SOURCE 31

Non-co-operation aims at the overthrow of the government and is legally seditious.

Gandhi, *Young India*, 1922

SOURCE 32

I came to the conclusion that the British connection made India more helpless than she ever was before, politically and economically.

SOURCE 33

It is impossible to ignore the fact that you are in a different category from any person I have ever tried, or am likely to try . . . . in the eyes of millions of your countrymen, you are a great leader and patriot.

Judge Broomfield, 1922, quoted in D. Byrne, Mahatma Gandhi, 1984

In sentencing Gandhi, the Judge admitted that he was a special case (Source 33). Nevertheless, Gandhi was sentenced to six years in prison! He did not serve his whole sentence. After two years he fell ill with appendicitis — was operated upon — and was later released. The British did not wish Gandhi to die whilst he was their captive.

Between 1928 and 1930 Indian nationalists' hopes for home rule were first raised by Britain and then dashed.

GANDHI'S ACTION: 'CIVIL DISOBEDIENCE' 1930

In protest against Britain's unwillingness to promote self-government for India — even at some future date — Gandhi called upon all Indians to take part in a massive campaign of non-violent, yet active, civil disobedience.

He explained his reasons in a letter to the British Viceroy (Source 34).

Source 35 illustrates the first act of Gandhi's campaign. He marched with thousands of followers 400 kilometres to the coast, where he picked up salt on the seashore. The heat of India's climate makes taking salt a necessity of life. Yet, despite being almost surrounded by salt water the Indians had no control over the production of salt. The British had total control, and everybody, rich or poor, had to pay a tax on it. By his simple act on the seashore Gandhi was actually breaking the law — he was avoiding payment of the salt tax.

Gandhi's act was the signal for other Indians to make their own salt and break the law.

SOURCE 34

I hold the British rule in India to be a curse. It has impoverished millions by a system of exploitation and by ruinously expensive military and civil administration. It has reduced us politically to serfdom. . . . nothing but organised non-violence can check the organised violence of the British government.

Gandhi, 1930, quoted in F. W. Rawding, *Gandhi*, 1980

SOURCE 35 Gandhi collects salt — a scene from the film *Gandhi*

BRITISH REACTION: At first the British were unconcerned about Gandhi's action. But Gandhi's act, so simple yet so symbolic of India's dependence on Britain, captured the imagination of millions. It received massive publicity through newspapers and newsreels.

Indians staged acts of non-violent protest around the country. At Dharasana salt depot, as you've already seen, they tried to get into the factory to protest about all salt production being in government hands. The British were forced to act. During the next few months over 60,000 Indians were imprisoned. Gandhi was amongst them, and this time there was no trial (Source 36).

Yet the civil disobedience campaign was successful. Many people in both Britain and India began to realise that Britain could not hold India by force. Many people were shocked at Britain's heavy-handed response to the non-violent protest. The publicity harmed Britain's image and reputation as a humane world power. Some British politicians began to think in terms of Indian self-government. Indians now began to believe that one day they could win their independence.

SOURCE 36 Gandhi arrested and imprisoned without trial – a scene from the film *Gandhi*

EVENTS: 1931 CONFERENCE Gandhi was released from prison and invited to a series of meetings with the Viceroy. He was then invited to attend a conference in 1931 in London.

The conference itself was a failure for India – independence was still not promised. Gandhi predicted as much before he sailed for Britain (Source 37).

SOURCE 37

The elephant is powerless to think in terms of the ant, and the Englishman is powerless to think in terms of the Indian.

Gandhi, 1931, quoted in D. Byrne, *Mahatma Gandhi*, 1984

GANDHI'S ACTION: BRITAIN 1931 — While in Britain Gandhi travelled north to Lancashire to meet cotton mill workers (Source 38). His campaign to boycott imported cloth meant many Lancashire workers had lost their jobs. They nevertheless greeted him with affection.

SOURCE 38 Gandhi with textile workers in Lancashire, 1931

BRITISH REACTION: 1932 — Gandhi returned to India as a hero. But to the British he remained a dangerous enemy. Eventually, in 1932, he was arrested and imprisoned again — without trial — along with over 30,000 followers.

GANDHI'S ACTION: — While in prison Gandhi learned of a British plan to divide up India's voters on the basis of religion. He announced his decision to fast to death unless Britain withdrew the plan.

BRITISH REACTION: — Gandhi was now over 60. The British feared the consequences if Gandhi were to die as a martyr in prison, and so dropped their plans.

EVENT: 1939 SECOND WORLD WAR — In 1939 Britain and the Empire entered the Second World War against Germany.

GANDHI'S ACTION: — Gandhi resisted the temptation to press hard for Indian independence at a time when Britain was most vulnerable.

BRITISH REACTION: — In return for active Indian support in the war, Britain promised India internal self-government as soon as the war ended — but not full independence. Winston Churchill, Britain's Prime Minister, wanted to keep the Empire together (Source 39).

SOURCE 39

I have not become the King's first minister to preside over the liquidation of the Empire.

◄ Winston Churchill, 1940, quoted in F. W. Rawding, *Gandhi*, 1980

GANDHI'S ACTION: 'QUIT INDIA!' 1942	Gandhi objected to Britain's ideas for self-government because they allowed individual religious groups to work out separate deals with Britain. Gandhi saw his vision of 'one India' being ruined by the desire of some Indian Muslims to create their own separate state. In July 1942 Gandhi drew up the 'Quit India!' plan. In it the Congress Party declared that: 'British rule in India must cease immediately'.
BRITISH REACTION:	Britain had no intention of quitting India. Swiftly, Gandhi and other Congress Party leaders were arrested.
EVENTS: VIOLENCE	Violence broke out all over India. Symbols of British rule, like post offices, railway stations and government offices, were attacked. Murders and lootings began.
GANDHI'S ACTION:	For once, Gandhi, still in gaol, was unable to stop the violence. He tried, by staging a 21-day fast, but with no success.
BRITISH REACTION:	The British blamed Gandhi for the disorder. They now seemed willing to let him die in prison. Eventually, in 1944, aged 75, he was released on doctor's advice.
GANDHI'S ACTION:	He immediately set about trying to unite the Hindu and Muslim leaders in demanding one India. But Mohammed Jinnah, leader of the Muslim League, wished to see a separate Muslim country as part of an agreement with the British. Gandhi was unable to unite the two sides.
BRITISH REACTION: 1945	By 1945 the war against Germany and Japan was over. A newly elected government in Britain announced its intention to give India independence. Plans were drawn up to resolve the complicated problems of Hindu–Muslim disunity.

EVENT: 'DIRECT ACTION' 1946

In August 1946 Jinnah called on Muslims to take 'direct action' to demand an independent Muslim state, to be called Pakistan.

Violence erupted (see Source 40). Muslim killed Hindu. Hindu killed Muslim. In one day alone 5000 people died in Calcutta. India was in a state of civil war.

SOURCE 40 Corpses in Calcutta, August 1946

GANDHI'S ACTION:	Gandhi went to Calcutta. Later he toured both Muslim and Hindu villages to try to calm the unrest.

BRITISH REACTION:	Still the violence continued. In February 1947 the British Government announced that it would give up the government of India by June 1948. The last Viceroy — Lord Mountbatten — arrived. He consulted regularly with Gandhi, Jinnah and Nehru (leader of the Congress Party).
EVENTS: PARTITION	Rather than risk full civil war Gandhi and Nehru accepted Jinnah's demands. India would be split — partitioned — to create a Muslim 'Pakistan' separate from the predominantly Hindu 'India'. The partition was no simple matter. States such as Bengal and the Punjab which had large numbers of Hindus and Muslims had to be somehow divided.
INDEPENDENCE 1947	India gained independence on 15th August 1947 (see Source 41). Nehru became India's first Prime Minister. One day earlier Pakistan had also become independent. **SOURCE 41** Lord Mountbatten's carriage at the Independence celebrations

GANDHI'S ACTION:	Gandhi was not present at the independence celebrations. He stayed in Calcutta to try to stop the religious violence.
EVENTS: CONFLICT	Following independence, violence broke out once again, as large numbers of Muslims realised they were going to be under Hindu rule, or Hindus under Muslim rule. Millions of refugees fled from one new country to the other. Half a million people were killed in the religious hatred.
GANDHI'S ACTION:	Once again Gandhi announced he would fast. He would not stop until it was safe for Muslims to walk the streets of Delhi. The violence in Delhi did subside. But by supporting the rights of Muslims Gandhi had put his own life in danger. Fanatical Hindus plotted to kill him.
EVENT: ASSASSINATION	On 30th January 1948 Gandhi walked through a large crowd which had gathered to hear him. In the crowd was a young assassin. As Gandhi approached, the young man bowed, then fired. Gandhi fell and died. That night, Nehru broadcast to the nation (see Source 42).

SOURCE 42

The light has gone out of our lives and there is darkness everywhere. Our beloved leader . . . the father of our nation, is no more.

Nehru, 1948, quoted in F. W. Rawding, Gandhi, 1980

Explain, using one or two sentences, what part each of the following played in Gandhi's thinking:
a The spinning wheel (self-sufficiency)
b Non-violence
c Non-co-operation
d Civil disobedience
e Hindu–Muslim unity

INDEPENDENCE IN AFRICA

The achievement of Indian independence is an early example of a process known as DECOLONISATION. After 1945 millions of people in colonies began to demand the freedom to act, make decisions and run their own countries without interference from others.

Source 43 shows the speed of decolonisation in Africa. This transformation was noted in a famous speech made in 1960 by the British Prime Minister, Harold Macmillan (see Source 44).

SOURCE 44

In the 20th century we have seen the awakening of national consciousness in people who have lived for centuries in dependence on some other power. The wind of change is blowing through the continent.

Africa provides a good example for us to look, briefly, at four important questions to do with decolonisation.

1 Were all the colonial powers unpopular for the same reason?

There were major differences in the ways in which the four main colonial powers in Africa treated their colonies. *Britain* thought of itself as a parent — the mother country — helping a child to develop. One day Britain's African colonies would be able to look after themselves. Often Britain allowed tribal chiefs to rule with the aid of British advisers.

France believed its mission was to make Africans into Frenchmen. The French colonies were run from Paris and treated as though part of France. *Belgium* and *Portugal* ruled their colonies very harshly — they saw little value in transferring power to the African people.

SOURCE 43 The decolonisation of Africa

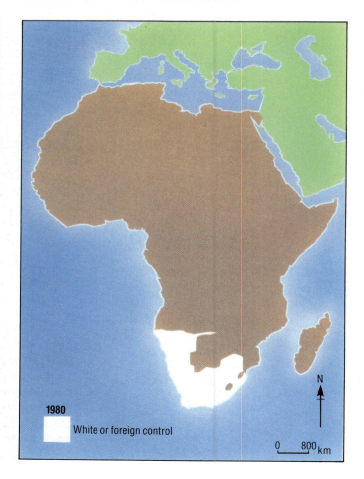

1945 — White or foreign control — 0 800 km

1980 — White or foreign control — 0 800 km

2 What part did the Second World War play?

The events of 1939–1945 played an important part in the move towards decolonisation By 1945 countries like Britain and France no longer had the strength, nor wealth, to hold on to their African colonies against the will of African nationalists. Many Africans had fought in the Allied armies. They had learnt about European ideas and had seen the differences in living standards between Europe and Africa.

Africans wondered why they had fought Nazi Germany to defend freedom, when their own countries were not yet free. Others saw how easily their colonial 'masters' had been defeated by the Japanese in the Far East and realised that because of the war the main colonial powers were exhausted.

Lastly, after 1945 the world was dominated by new 'masters' – the USA and the USSR. Both superpowers disliked the idea of colonies and, in different ways, pressured the old colonial powers to give up their overseas empires.

Indian independence in 1947 set the scene for the rest of Asia and for Africa. Once some countries were given independence, others wanted it too. Source 45 shows the success of the independence movement in Africa.

SOURCE 45 Africa: the progress towards independence

UK
BELGIUM
FRANCE
ITALY
PORTUGAL SPAIN
TUNISIA 1956
MOROCCO 1956
ALGERIA 1962
LIBYA 1951
EGYPT 1922
WEST SAHARA 1975
An independent kingdom until captured by Italians in 1935
MAURITANIA 1960
MALI 1960
NIGER 1960
CHAD 1960
SUDAN 1956
DJIBOUTI 1977
SENEGAL 1960
GAMBIA 1965
GUINEA BISSAU 1974
GUINEA 1958
SIERRA LEONE 1961
IVORY COAST 1960
NIGERIA 1960
CAMEROON 1960-61
CENT-AFRICAN REP 1960
ETHIOPIA 1941
SOMALIA 1960
BENIN 1960
BURKINA FASO 1960
TOGO 1960
GHANA 1957
UGANDA 1962
KENYA 1963
RWANDA 1962
BURUNDI 1962
LIBERIA 1847 (the only completely independent African country in 1939)
EQUATORIAL GUINEA 1968
GABON 1960
CONGO 1960
ZAIRE 1960
TANZANIA 1961-1963
ANGOLA 1976
ZAMBIA 1964
MOZAMBIQUE 1975
MALAWI 1964
MADAGASCAR 1960
NAMIBIA
BOTSWANA 1966
ZIMBABWE 1980
SOUTH AFRICA 1910
SWAZILAND 1968
LESOTHO 1966

0   1000 Kilometres

1960 Date of independence

Independent nations in 1939 but with strong British ties

Countries governing a neighbouring country

N

3 How was the transfer of power achieved?

In the British colonies the transfer of power went fairly smoothly. Newly independent nations were invited to retain important links with Britain through membership of the Commonwealth, and many did so.

Elsewhere other European colonial powers were reluctant to give up their possessions. Portugal's determination to hang on to Angola and Mozambique resulted in a long guerrilla war between African nationalists and Portuguese troops.

SOURCE 46 A Nigerian soldier captured by Biafran troops during the Civil War, 1967

SOURCE 47 Jomo Kenyatta of Kenya

4 What difficulties have independent African nations had to face?

The recent history of many African states has been far from peaceful. Many newly independent nations have found that freedom has produced its difficulties as well as its benefits. Upon independence all wished to develop into democracies, but each nation has been faced with problems along the way.

Some problems arose because the frontiers of the countries had been drawn up in the colonial era as lines on a map, which paid little attention to important natural barriers like mountains and rivers.

Even less notice was taken in the 19th century of the tribal areas, which had existed for centuries. Peoples or tribes were often split between one country and another. A country might contain different tribes – who in the past might have been enemies. Trying to create a sense of unity in such circumstances has been very difficult. Often rivalries between tribes have flared up into bloody civil wars, such as in Nigeria in the 1960s (see Source 46).

Another problem was that some European powers failed to spend enough time preparing black Africans to take over power. If independence was granted too quickly the chaos which followed could lead to civil war. This happened in the Congo (Zaire) when Belgium suddenly withdrew.

Some African nations have experienced long periods of peaceful stable democratic government – with respected nationalist leaders such as Jomo Kenyatta in Kenya (Source 47) – but other countries have suffered from frequent changes of government. In many cases democracy has been replaced by military rule – 22 out of the 38 governments in Africa are army backed. Some nations have military dictatorships. Elsewhere, countries like Tanzania have seen Communism as the best way forward, often looking to the USSR or China for aid.

The offers of aid for development from the superpowers have created their own pressures, since many African countries wish to be NON-ALIGNED rather than be seen to support either the East or the West.

Perhaps the greatest problem the newly independent nations have had to face is poverty. Of the 25 poorest countries in the world, 17 are in Africa. Although Europe is no longer Africa's political master, the patterns of agriculture, industry and trade set up in the colonial era may still remain. The economies of the new nations are often dominated by the old colonial powers. This NEO-COLONIALISM restricts truly independent development and has created serious problems for African politicians.

ASSESSMENT

Cause and consequence

1 The chart below gives a list of the main elements in the colonial system. Some elements are supplied by the 'mother country', e.g. Britain, and some by the colony, e.g. India.

  a In pairs, draw up a table putting the items in the list under the correct heading, 'mother country' or 'colony'.

  b Now, individually, use the elements to help you write a paragraph explaining clearly the relationship between the mother country and the colony in the colonial system.

  c Compare your paragraph with your partner's. Are they the same? Do you feel your explanation is biased? Is your partner's? Are they biased in the same way? Do you think it is possible to write a totally unbiased account of colonialism?

The main elements in the colonial system

A Large numbers of people, for cheap labour
B A large fleet of cargo-carrying merchant ships
C A desire to create wealth by profits from trade
D A capacity to mass-produce manufacturing goods
E Plentiful raw materials
F A strong navy to protect trade routes
G An efficient, well-equipped army to enforce order
H Businesses with wealth to invest in new ideas for goods
I A vast population to sell manufactured goods to
J The technology to extract and transport raw materials
K An efficient and well-established class of administrators
L Weak central government
M An economy based on agriculture and domestic industry rather than mass-production

---

Role of the individual

2a To what extent did Gandhi's actions control events?

  b To what extent did events control Gandhi's actions? Give examples to support your ideas.

  c Do you think Gandhi was successful because he depended on non-violence? Explain your answer.

SOURCE 48

No people exists that would not think itself happier under its own bad government than it might really be under the good government of an alien [foreign] power.

Utility

3 Look at what Gandhi said in 1905 about colonialism (Source 48). Write four short paragraphs saying whether you agree with this view. You might divide your writing up under the following headings:

● Benefits of colonialism for those being governed
● Disadvantages of colonialism for those being governed
● Advantages of independence
● Problems of self-government

Use examples from India, Africa and any other colonised country, where possible.

9

Multi-cultural Britain

WHO ARE THE BRITISH?

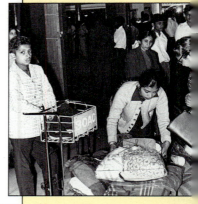

SOURCE 1 *Stone Age*
A flint blade. Blades like this one were used by Old Stone Age peoples who migrated to Britain over 40,000 years ago.

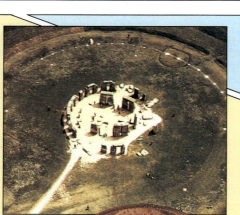

SOURCE 2 *Bronze Age*
Stonehenge – built over 3000 years ago by people who came to Britain from present-day Holland and Germany.

SOURCE 12 *Late twentieth century* Asian immigrants, London Airport. Many arrived from India, Pakistan and East Africa in the 1960s and 1970s.

SOURCE 3 *Iron Age*
A Celtic mirror. The Celts came to Britain between the seventh and first centuries BC.

SOURCE 4 *Roman*
Model of a Roman soldier. The Romans invaded Britain in AD 43, but did not colonise Britain in large numbers.

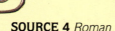

SOURCE 5 *Saxon*
Belt buckle found at Sutton Hoo. The Anglo-Saxons settled in Britain from about AD 450 and forced the Celts to move westwards.

SOURCE 6 *Vikings*
A dragon's head from a Viking long ship. The Vikings first raided Britain, but later settled here.

SOURCE 11 *Mid-twentieth century*

Immigrants from the West Indies arrive in Southampton, 1961. During the Second World War, when Britain was short of workers, people from the colonies were encouraged to migrate to Britain. At the end of the war many West Indians stayed in Britain, and in the 1950s and 1960s more West Indians joined them.

SOURCE 10 *Early twentieth century*

Jewish actor outside a Jewish cinema in the East End of London. Before the First World War thousands of Jews came to Britain fleeing persecution in Eastern Europe. In the 1930s, Poles, Czechs, Austrians and Germans migrated to Britain to escape Hitler's Nazi dictatorship.

SOURCE 9 *Nineteenth century*

A priest blessing Irish peasants about to emigrate, 1851. Thousands of Irish moved from their home country to other parts of the British Isles.

SOURCE 8 *Sixteenth and seventeenh centuries*

In the sixteenth and seventeenth centuries Dutch, Flemish and French Protestants came to Britain to escape religious persecution.

SOURCE 7 *Normans*

The Bayeux Tapestry. After the Norman Conquest in 1066 King William rewarded his Norman followers with land and property.

The British people are the result of thousands of years of migration. Migration is not simply movement between countries. There is also movement within countries.

See if each of you can trace the movements of your family. Make a note of your own place of birth, that of your parents, and your grandparents. Has there been any movement about the country, or between countries, in the last three generations of your family?

Share your findings with the rest of the class. Perhaps you could plot all your information on to a large map, each of you pinning a flag to indicate where you, your parents and your grandparents were born. You will then be able to see at a glance just how much migration there has been.

AIMS

This unit will help you see that Britain is a *multi-cultural* society. It is made up of a variety of different people, with different religions, languages and backgrounds. This DIVERSITY has come about as a result of IMMIGRATION over thousands of years.

You will be looking at some of the causes of immigration and the reasons why two particular groups of immigrants decided to come to Britain. Immigrants have settled in all parts of Britain. In this unit, though, we shall be looking at just one city — London. How did people already living there react to the new arrivals? How have the immigrants themselves felt about their new country?

IRISH IMMIGRANTS IN 19th-CENTURY LONDON

London – a magnet for migrants

Over hundreds of years London has received many different groups of immigrants – Huguenots (French Protestants), Irish, Jews, West Indians and Asians, among many others. Some parts of London – such as the Spitalfields area – have seen several different groups of immigrants coming and going over the years. In 1978 a survey by the Inner London Education Authority discovered that over 130 different languages were spoken by its pupils. The 12 most spoken languages (other than English) provide clues to the origins of London's 20th-century immigrants – Bengali, Turkish, Spanish, Gujarati, Punjabi, Greek, Italian, Urdu, Chinese, French, Arabic and Portuguese.

> 1 In pairs, make a list of all the advantages a big city like London might offer immigrants to Britain.
>
> 2 Now make a list of any disadvantages you can think of.

SOURCE 14 Irish emigrants waiting on the quayside before boarding ships sailing for Liverpool, 1851

Why did the Irish come?

Source 13 shows the number of Irish who migrated to other parts of the British Isles over the last two hundred years. During the 19th century, the peak years for Irish emigration were the 1840s and 1850s. One and a half million Irish emigrated between 1841 and 1851.

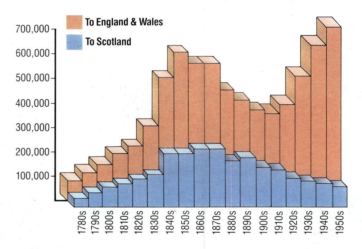

SOURCE 13 Irish migration to Britain, 1780–1980

Push and pull factors

In pairs study Sources 15–20, together with their captions. They provide clues as to some of the reasons why the Irish migrated.

Historians usually divide the causes of migration into 'push' factors and 'pull' factors. 'Push' factors occur in the person's home country. They are things which have the effect of 'pushing' the person out. 'Pull' factors are things about the new country that might attract an immigrant. When you have examined the sources:

1 List the reasons why so many Irish migrated to England in the nineteenth century.

2 Divide the list into 'push' and 'pull' factors.

3 Explain what was the *single* most important cause of this mass migration.

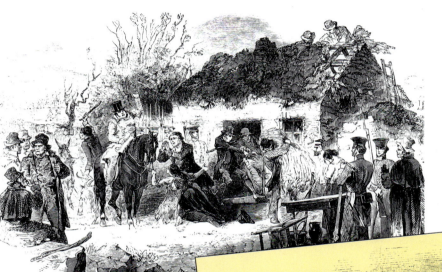

SOURCE 15 A crisis in Irish farming in the mid-nineteenth century left many peasants unable to afford their rents. Here a tenant family is evicted by its landlord

SOURCE 16 In the mid-nineteenth century many of Britain's new railway lines were built with the aid of 'navvies' — many of whom were Irish immigrants. This print shows a bridge and cutting under construction on the Eastern Union Railway, 1846

SOURCE 17 Victims of the Irish potato famine are pulled away by cart: Cork, 1847

In desperation, people ate dandelion roots, leaves and nuts, berries, nettles and even the bark from trees. But nothing could ward off starvation. In 1847 William Bennett described the scene he found at Belmullet, County Mayo (Source 19).

SOURCE 20 Children who survived the potato famine were often left in desperate situations. Print from the *Illustrated London News*, 1847

Settling in London

Source 21 shows the Rookery of St Giles, where large numbers of Irish immigrants settled. By 1840 there were already more than 10,000 Irish living in this small area. An eye witness wrote a description of the Rookery (Source 22).

SOURCE 21 A nineteenth-century street scene in an Irish area of London

1 List the problems of city life faced by a newly arrived Irish immigrant.

2 What picture of Irish immigrants do Sources 21 and 22 conjure up?

3 How far does the description (Source 22) agree with the print (Source 21)?

4 How do you think the English people at the time might have felt about Irish immigrants?

St Giles had problems of dirt, overcrowding, disease and crime. Many thousands of people lived in damp, airless cellars, without light or ventilation. There was no clean water, no proper sewage system and no refuse collection. It is little wonder that disease was widespread. Many people died, especially the very young and the elderly.

Despite such difficulties, many Irish immigrants did what they could. Henry Mayhew investigated the street life of London and its poor in the late 19th century. He wrote about an area of the East End where many Irish lived (Source 23).

SOURCE 23

In all the houses that I entered were traces of household care . . . that I had little expected. The cupboard . . . stocked with mugs, the mantlepiece with its images, the walls covered with . . . prints of Saints and Martyrs, gave an air of comfort.

Henry Mayhew, *London Labour and the London Poor, 1861*

SOURCE 22

Rows of crumbling houses . . . in which the wretchedness of London takes shelter. Squalid children, haggard men with long uncombed hair in rags . . . many speaking Irish, women without shoes – a babe at the breast with a single garment confined to the waist by a bit of string; wolfish looking dogs; decayed vegetables strewing the pavement, low public houses, linen hanging across the street to dry . . .

M. Fore, On the Dwellings of the Poor, *1851*

1 How does the picture painted by Source 23 differ from the one painted by Source 22?

2 Must one of the writers be lying or mistaken?

3 How do you explain the difference?

4 Source 23 provides a clue as to why some of the English might have disliked the Irish. Can you spot it?

How did the English react to the Irish?

Many of the English inhabitants of London and elsewhere disliked their new Irish neighbours. Why was this?

Religion

In the 18th century there were already 140,000 Irish in Britain. They were devoted Catholics in a fiercely Protestant country. In 1780 the Gordon Riots took place in London. Angry Protestants rampaged through the streets, burning and destroying Catholic property, and calling for 'no popery'. The Irish were picked out as a special target for attack.

By the 19th century there was less religious persecution of the Irish. But the English and Irish were still suspicious of each other's religions.

Different customs

The English misunderstood certain Irish customs and habits, and found them disgusting. The Irish 'wake' or funeral party was one such custom (see Source 24). Bodies stayed unburied for some days in order to give relatives a chance to get together and mourn the dead. A doctor wrote about what he found when he visited an Irish house after the death of an inhabitant (Source 25).

The English also disliked the way the Irish kept animals, like pigs, in their living rooms, or left them to scavenge in the streets. This was the way the Irish had been used to keeping animals back home in the Irish countryside. In London it certainly didn't help make the streets or homes any cleaner.

Employment

A third area of conflict concerned jobs. In the 18th century many Irish labourers came to Britain at harvest time and then returned home. But in the 19th century they came to settle permanently, mostly in the industrial towns and cities.

Many of London's Irish worked as dockers at the Port of London. But dock work had its ups and downs. Henry Mayhew described a scene at the dock gates in 1861 (Source 26).

> **SOURCE 26**
>
> *Now the appeal [for work from the foreman] is made in Irish blarney – the scuffle being made the fiercer by the knowledge that hundreds must be left to idle the day out in want.*
>
> *Henry Mayhew,* London Labour and the London Poor, *1861*

The Irish could not always find regular work. This made the English view them as idle and drunk. As more and more people took this view the Irish immigrants found it even harder to get work. They were often faced with large notices: 'NO IRISH NEED APPLY'.

If the men could not find employment, the women had to go out to work. Many Irish women became domestic servants, while others took to selling fruit in the streets. One orange-seller quoted by Henry Mayhew described her desperation (Source 27).

> **SOURCE 27**
>
> **We don't live, we starve. We git a few taties. Today I've not take 3d [2p] as yet, Sir and it's past three. . . . We live accordingly for there's 1s. 3d. [7p] a week for rent. . . . I don't know what will become of us if times don't turn.**

SOURCE 24
Irish funeral wake, 1882

> **SOURCE 25**
>
> *. . . a horrible stench arose from a corpse which had died . . . 12 days before, and the coffin stood across the foot of the bed. This was a small room, and a fire always in it . . . being the only one for sleeping, living and eating in.*
>
> Report on . . . the Practice of Interment in Towns, *1843*

Irish men could easily work as railway navvies, though. Many English workers were unwilling to leave their home parish. Irish men, on the other hand, were prepared to live in temporary 'shanties' in remote places and to wander around the country looking for work.

Crime and disease

In the 19th century the Irish were blamed for many of the social problems in Britain's cities. London's growing crime rate was blamed on them. The Irish were also accused of spreading disease because the areas they lived in were so crowded and insanitary – without proper drainage or sewerage (see Source 28). Typhus – a disease which was common in filthy slums – was known as 'Irish fever'.

It did seem at times as though the Irish were blamed for everything that went wrong. In 1862 an Irish woman described her sense of frustration and misery at the way in which everything and everybody seemed to be against her (Source 29).

1 List all the problems blamed on the Irish.

2 What, do you think, was the single most important reason why the English disliked the Irish? Explain your choice.

3 Why do you think so many English people were keen to blame the Irish for all their problems?

In general, despite English resentment of them, the Irish mixed into 19th-century British society without a major upheaval. There were occasional 'randies' or pitched battles, between Irish navvies and their English and Scottish counterparts, but no major riots occurred in the big cities. This was partly because the middle of the 19th century was a prosperous time for England. The Industrial Revolution had created a huge demand for cheap, unskilled labour.

Also, there was no real evidence that the Irish were any more to blame for the social problems than millions of British working-class people who lived in similar dirty, overcrowded conditions.

When the English actually met the Irish and got to know them, they were often impressed by what they discovered. A Birmingham plasterer, John Holmes, wrote of how his views changed (Source 30).

Above all, once they had lived here for some time, it was impossible to tell an Irish person from an English one. Their language, dress and physical appearance were identical.

English dislike of the Irish immigrants was based mainly on PREJUDICE. Their opinion of the Irish was based on fear and ignorance rather than knowledge and reason. They were suspicious of the Irish because they seemed different.

a Why might English workers have been afraid of Irish immigrants?

b The Irish tended to live together in the same areas of the cities rather than mixing with the English. Why do you think this was?

c As time passed, the prejudice lessened. Is there still some prejudice against the Irish in England today? If so, how does the prejudice show itself?

d If prejudice is based on fear and ignorance, what is the best way of overcoming it? Discuss this with a partner, and then share your views with the rest of the class.

BENGALI IMMIGRANTS IN 20th-CENTURY LONDON

Look at Source 31. It shows Bengali children (children from Bangladesh) in London's East End in the 1970s. Many Asian immigrants — some from Bangladesh (see Source 32) — have come to Britain in the last 30 years. As Source 31 shows, many of these immigrants are crowded into older, poor quality, inner-city housing. One such area in East London is around Spitalfields and Brick Lane. Over the centuries the area has received French, Irish, Jewish and now Bengali immigrants.

1 Are there any clues from Source 31 that these Bengalis have retained cultural links with Bangladesh?

2 Like the Irish in the 19th century, the Bengali immigrants tend to live together in their own separate communities. Why do you think this is?

SOURCE 31 Bengali children in East London

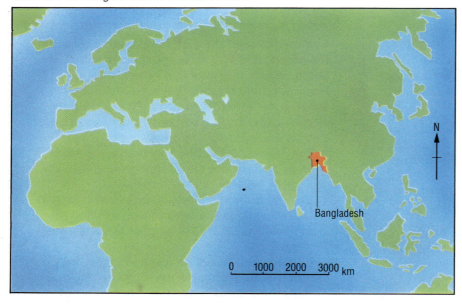

SOURCE 32 The location of Bangladesh

Why have the Bengalis come?

Since the early days of British rule in India (see Unit 8), Bengali sailors have come to London. Many worked as cooks or galley-hands on board British ships. These Indian sailors were called lascars (see Source 33).

In between voyages, many of the lascars settled in London and took up a variety of shorebased jobs. Some, for instance, ran lodging houses for fellow seamen, while others set up tea-houses and cafés along the water front. Yet others traded in the street markets.

During the First World War Britain's large Merchant Navy was short of manpower. Many Bengalis were recruited. When they left the navy, some settled in London's East End. Slowly the Spitalfields—Brick Lane area became the centre of a growing Bengali community.

But the real influx of Bengalis came after the Second World War. There were several reasons, which included 'push' as well as 'pull' factors.

SOURCE 33 Lascar seamen at work on a British ship

Push factors

1) In 1947 the British left India, and the country was split up to form the Hindu state of India and the Muslim state of West and East Pakistan. The Bengali sailors lived in what was now called East Pakistan. However, their main port, Calcutta, was just across the new border, in India. They feared they might lose their sea-faring jobs. Many of them therefore decided to settle in Britain permanently.

2) Pakistan's two parts, East and West, were separated by thousands of miles of Indian territory. The Bengalis in East Pakistan grew impatient with their government in the West. In 1971 there was a civil war. East Pakistan became an independent state known as Bangladesh (meaning Bengal State). The civil war produced misery and homelessness which persuaded many Bengalis to emigrate.

3) Bangladesh suffered from cyclones, floods and famines. There was much poverty. In the early 1970s Bangladesh had only one doctor to every 9000 people, one hospital bed to every 7000 people, and one teacher to every 50 students. Many Bengalis saw emigration as their only hope of escaping this poverty.

Pull factors

1) Britain had a shortage of workers in certain jobs at the end of the Second World War. Immigrants from countries of the 'New Commonwealth' like India and Pakistan were welcomed.

2) A British Nationalities Act in 1948 declared Commonwealth citizens to be 'Citizens of the UK and the Colonies'. As British passport holders, the Bengalis had the right to come to Britain to live. So those who settled down started bringing relations and others to support them in their business and commercial ventures.

The early Bengali immigrants were relatively few in number. They were mostly men and could speak some English. After 1960 this pattern changed. By the 1970s, Spitalfields' immigrants came mainly from small villages in Bangladesh. There were many more women and children. They brought their traditional way of life with them. Most could not speak English, nor did they know anything about British customs and culture.

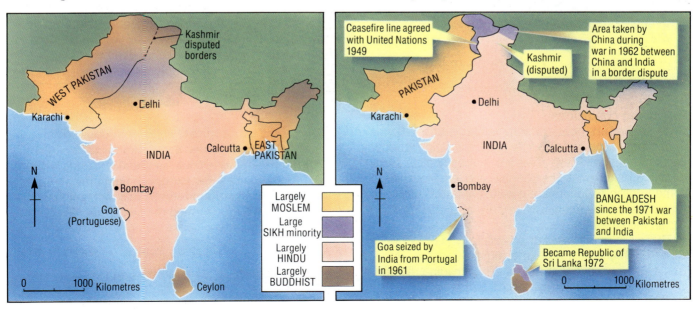

SOURCE 34 (a) The Indian sub-continent in 1947   (b) The Indian sub-continent since 1947

Living in Spitalfields

The Spitalfields–Brick Lane area suffers from poor housing and lack of amenities. These problems are common to many of Britain's inner-city areas.

SOURCE 35 East End housing, London, 1983

For many immigrants from Bangladesh, London's dirty back streets are a far cry from the country they left behind. Compare Source 35 with Source 36, a description of the remote rural district of Sylhet — where many of Britain's Bengali population once lived.

> ### SOURCE 36
>
> *The Bengali people . . . in the East End . . . are very romantic about Sylhet and Bangladesh. It's a land of great wide rivers, and boats, of enormously beautiful sunsets . . . a rich land on which . . . there are two or three crops a year on the same . . . land.*
>
> D. Jones, *Asian Links, 1982*

Bad living conditions

Because they are poor and new to this country, Bengali immigrants have had to settle in derelict and run-down parts of London. These areas were already dirty and decaying long before the Bengalis arrived. However, some English residents are now blaming this decay on the arrival of the Bengalis. They are also blaming them for an increase in disease.

There are many cases of tuberculosis (TB) in the East End. Many of those suffering are Bengalis. But this does not prove that Asians are spreading disease. TB is usually connected with cold, damp living conditions. All it shows is that Bengalis live in some of the worst and most insanitary housing in the area.

Employment

The Irish were fortunate to arrive in Britain at a time when jobs were plentiful. The Bengalis have not been so lucky. The 1960s were prosperous years with full employment. By the 1980s, some old industries had

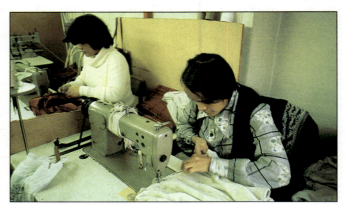

SOURCE 37 Bengali women at work in the East End, 1982

run down and unemployment had risen. About one tenth of the workforce is out of work (1989). Many Bengalis have been unable to find work. The unemployment rate among Asian men is double that for white men. Other Bengalis have been forced to take 'sweated' jobs. For example, many Bengali residents of Spitalfields are employed in small clothing firms, often working very long hours, in unhealthy surroundings, for poor pay (see Source 37).

Some Bengalis have broken out of this 'poverty trap'. They have set up businesses of their own. They are very succcessful at running restaurants (see Source 38). About 80% of the Indian and Pakistani restaurants in Britain are run by people from Bangladesh. The British people have welcomed Indian food into their way of life (see Source 39).

> ### SOURCE 39
>
> One of the extraordinary changes in domestic life, in the short span of one generation, is that exotic cuisine [food] has become so popular. Along with the Chinese and some European immigrants, Indians have revolutionised British eating habits . . . and have transformed the face of the local high-streets.
>
> J. Walvin, *Passage to Britain*, 1984

Many Bengalis have achieved some prosperity and success by working very hard and showing good

SOURCE 38 An East End Indian restaurant, 1988

business sense. But because of the high unemployment they still find it difficult to gain acceptance, whether out of work or running successful businesses. Unemployed Bengalis are often accused of being 'lazy' and 'living off the state'. Those with jobs are often blamed for 'taking the jobs of English people'. It seems that the Bengali immigrants, like the Irish, just cannot win.

Some Bengalis have become quite wealthy through hard work and good management. They no longer live in poverty. Yet some non-Asian people resent them all the more because of their success. Try to explain why.

Religion
Like the Irish before them, the Bengalis have brought their own religion with them to Britain. They have been determined to preserve both their Muslim faith and their separate language.

For Bengalis their language provides a link with their successful struggle for independence from Pakistan in 1971 (see Source 40).

The language is kept alive by numerous newspapers printed in Bengali and by Bengali films in cinemas (see Source 41).

Some people claim that if Bengalis insist on keeping their own language and religion they will never become integrated into British life. But Bengali leaders disagree. They claim that by keeping their religion and identity, Bengalis are certain to be good citizens (see Source 42).

SOURCE 40

Every Bengali thinks that he or she bears the heritage of predecessors who gave their life for the cause of the language. It's as important as bread and butter, clothes and shelter. I can't say more than that.

Anowara Jehan,
Asian Links, 1982

SOURCE 42

Islam is not only a religion, it's a complete code of life. To be a good Muslim will help them to be . . . part and parcel of this multi-racial society . . . and to abide by the law of this country.

Abdur Ruzzaq Siddiqui,
Asian Links, 1982

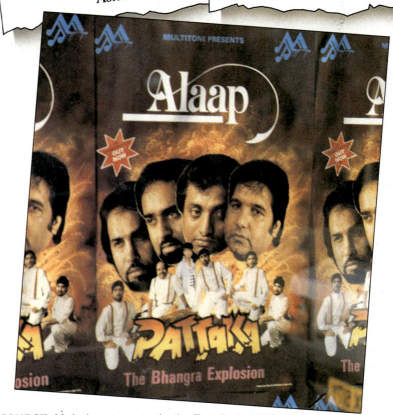

SOURCE 41 A cinema poster in the East End, 1988

1 Try to say, in your own words, why Bengalis want to retain their own language and faith.

2 Do you think it is easy or difficult for Bengalis to try to keep their own identity? What problems might young people, in particular, face? Discuss this question as a class.

Conflict

As we have seen, the Bengalis make a strong and positive contribution to the economic and cultural life of the East End of London. Despite this, the Bengalis have been targets for racial attacks. The incident reported in Source 43 was typical of the 1970s.

> **SOURCE 43**
>
> *We are bothered about our lives. White children kick us and scream abuse. Bottles are thrown. We are threatend by the* NATIONAL FRONT. *The other day my wife and I had a light bulb thrown at us while we were walking down the street.*
>
> *Muhammed Huque,* Daily Mail, *6th August 1978*

The police were unable to protect the Bengalis against these attacks. Asians and whites worked together to stage a series of demonstrations against racism in the East End of London (see Source 44). The Bengali community itself in East London has now taken measures to resist racial abuse. It has formed organisations such as the Bengali Action Group.

SOURCE 44 An anti-racist demonstration, East End, 1978

A multi-cultural nation

Each new group of immigrants to Britain has had to face opposition and prejudice on arrival. Hostility has simply been transferred from one immigrant group to the next. What is different about the most recent immigrants to Britain is that the colour of their skin makes them easy to identify.

The government has done something to try to combat prejudice. In 1976 it introduced the Race Relations Act which made certain kinds of racial discrimination illegal. Official bodies such as the Commission for Racial Equality work hard at educating the population and making Britain a fairer society.

But laws against racism can only achieve so much. Real freedom and equality depend on changing people's *attitudes* to race and colour. People need to see and accept that Britain has always been a multi-cultural society.

Each successive wave of immigrants has brought something new and different to this country. For example, the Huguenots (French Protestants) who fled to England in the seventeenth century gave a tremendous boost to the woollen and cotton spinning industry at that time. Jewish immigrants in the nineteenth century contributed to Britain's manufacturing and retail trade. Irish immigrants played a large part in building the railways.

The most recent immigrants are equally valuable to Britain (see Source 45).

> **SOURCE 45**
>
> **Britain could not live as she does without her coloured immigrants. The health service would break down; roughly 40 per cent of the doctors of British hospitals up to consultant level come from overseas; the greater part from India and Pakistan; about 17 per cent of the trainee nurses alone in England and Wales come from the Commonwealth.**
>
> *The Times, 1966*

But immigrants have not only added to the economic wealth of Britain. They have also made contributions to its literature, music, art, films, fashion and so on.

If a nation is to develop and grow, it must face new challenges and accept new influences. The most powerful country in the world today – the United States of America – is a massive melting pot. It is a nation of immigrants who have come from the four corners of the earth.

ASSESSMENT

Similarity and difference

1 Compare the causes of Irish immigration into Britain in the 19th century with the causes of Bengali immigration into Britain this century. Make two lists, one of the similarities and the other of the differences.

Cause and consequence

2 a Using the sources on Bengali and Irish immigration, write down as many reasons as you can discover why British residents have often been suspicious and resentful of later arrivals.

  b Have Bengali immigrants been resented for the same reasons as Irish immigrants or are there any additional reasons?

Cross-reference

3 Immigration, as you have seen, is something which has been taking place in Britain over a long period of time. Sources 1–12 summarise this and you have of course studied some of the earlier invasions and settlements in more detail in Books 1 and 2. Draw up a time chart from 2000 BC to the present day, showing when different people and cultures came to Britain. For each entry, try to include one or two sentences saying what changes they brought about and what contributions they made to the British way of life. Here is a sample entry:

Date	Invaders/Settlers	Contributions to British way of life
500 BC	Celts	They introduced the use of iron tools, weapons and household goods to Britain. They were also superb artists and craftsmen. Many of their descendants still show a particular flair for 'the arts' — especially literature, poetry and song.

Investigation

Investigate the importance of immigration in the area you live in. Visit the nearest town or city and make a list of all the shops, restaurants, cinemas, mosques, synagogues, churches and clubs which show the influence of different waves of immigrants. If you cannot visit in person, then the classified pages of the telephone directory and a good street map should enable you to do the job.

Do you think immigrants have added a lot, a reasonable amount, or very little to the wealth and culture of your area?

Try to think of food you enjoy or music you listen to which would not be available if it were not for immigrants. Make a class list.

To discuss

What part do you think the teaching of history in schools can play in helping people towards a better understanding of each other?

10

Violent attempts at change

Skyjack Sunday

SUNDAY, 6TH SEPTEMBER, 1970, has become known as 'Skyjack Sunday'. On that day the Popular Front for the Liberation of Palestine (PFLP) hijacked four airliners, one in West Germany, one in Switzerland and two in Holland. The PFLP was a terrorist organisation dedicated to destroying the state of Israel and returning the land to its previous Palestinian inhabitants.

The extracts from *The Times* (Sources 1, 2, 4, 6 and 7) record the course of events.

SOURCE 3 Leila Khaled, who boarded a Boeing 707 with two grenades hidden in her clothing. Miraculously both grenades failed to explode. She was overpowered by security guards.

SOURCE 1

Four hijackings over Western Europe – three succeeded and the other failed after a hijacker was shot dead in a gunfight over the North Sea – made yesterday the worst day for piracy in the history of civil aviation.

Monday, 7th September

SOURCE 2

One man was shot dead and three other people injured during an attempted hijacking yesterday afternoon of an El Al Boeing 707 airliner carrying 145 passengers. . . .

The dead man had attempted to enter the pilot's cabin armed with a pistol and accompanied by a woman carrying two hand grenades.

Mrs Fay Shenk, an American tourist-class passenger, said later: 'A man had a small pistol in his hand and rushed forward towards the first-class section and the flight deck. The girl also jumped up with a grenade in each hand and rushed after him. Next thing I heard some shots that sounded like a cap gun, but I discovered later they were real bullets.'

Passengers gave conflicting reports of what happened next but certainly in the first-class section an unidentified young man, possibly a security guard, grabbed the woman by the elbows and disarmed her.

Monday, 7th September

SOURCE 4

Palestine guerrillas yesterday hijacked a BOAC VC10 airliner from Bahrain to Beirut with 115 on board, about 25 of them children. They made it land on the same desert airfield in northern Jordan where a Swiss and an American airliner have been held since Sunday.

Thursday, 10th September

SOURCE 5 Arab 'guerrillas' celebrating the destruction of the three hijacked planes they blew up at Dawson's Field, Jordan. The planes were valued at $25 million.

SOURCE 6

Private negotiations today began to try to secure the release of 56 hostages – including eight Britons – who were still being held by the Palestinian guerrillas. The other 255 passengers from the three hijacked aircraft had left Jordan.

Yesterday the guerrillas blew up the three aircraft after releasing most of the passengers.

Monday, 14th September

SOURCE 7

Miss Leila Khaled, the Arab guerrilla, was flown out of Britain on her way to Cairo last night after an operation of masterly secrecy. On board the RAF Comet she flew first to Munich where the aircraft picked up three other Arab guerrillas freed by the West German authorities.

The Comet then flew to Zurich where the three guerrillas released by Switzerland were embarked. Meanwhile the last six hostages from the airliners hijacked to Jordan were arriving in New York.

Thursday, 1st October

These events warned the world that international terrorism had arrived and could win 'victories'. The hijackers had forced the governments of Britain, West Germany and Switzerland to give in to their demands. Other fanatics noted this success and hoped to repeat it in the future. Terrorism was here to stay. Over the following years the number of terrorist acts increased dramatically. According to the US State Department, the annual worldwide total rose from 302 in 1970 to 690 in 1985.

> 1 Look at the photograph of Leila Khaled (Source 3). What image of her does it give? Does it suggest she was a fanatical, bloodthirsty assassin or a romantic freedom fighter? Explain your answer.
>
> 2 The three aircraft were blown up (see Source 5) in full view of the world's press and television. Do you think the PFLP deliberately planned it this way and, if so, why?

AIMS

Hijackings, kidnappings and assassinations are nothing new. Terrorism is a centuries-old political weapon. Many of its methods have been improved and developed over the ages. But only recently have acts of terrorism become everyday events, especially in Western Europe and the Middle East.

This unit is about violence and terror as agents of change. It focuses on the ways in which different organisations around the world attempt to use terror to overthrow governments or to win other objectives which they could not hope to achieve by peaceful and democratic methods. It raises the question of whether the end justifies the means. Can the use of terror be excused if it is in a good cause? And who is to decide what is a good cause?

ACTIVITY

What is a terrorist?

Sources 8–20 are descriptions and illustrations of six historical events which clearly involved the use of violence and terror. Read them through carefully. Then draw up a table with two columns. In the first column describe each of the six events in your own words, and in the second column briefly say whether you think the people responsible for them were terrorists, giving reasons for your conclusions. Finally, discuss your ideas with the rest of the class and try to produce a class definition of a terrorist.

EVENT 1

On 28th June 1914, a young Serb nationalist, Gavrilo Princip, assassinated the heir to the Austrian throne, Archduke Ferdinand, and his wife at Sarajevo. Princip was not acting alone. He belonged to a secret society called 'Young Bosnia' which wanted independence for the Serbs in the Austrian Empire. The Archduke's death set in motion a train of events that resulted in the First World War. At his trial Princip described the assassination (Source 8) and defended his action (Source 9).

> **SOURCE 8**
>
> I fired twice at Ferdinand from a distance of four or five paces [see Source 10]. I raised my hand to commit suicide, but some policemen and officers seized me and struck me. . . . They took me away, covered with blood, to the police station.

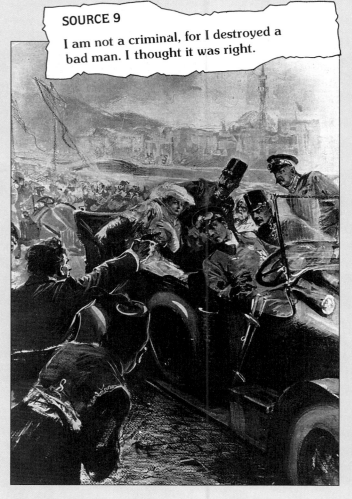

> **SOURCE 9**
>
> I am not a criminal, for I destroyed a bad man. I thought it was right.

SOURCE 10 Princip shot the Archduke in the neck and his wife in the stomach. They died almost instantly.

EVENT 2

During the Second World War members of the French Maquis (Resistance) waged a bitter struggle against the German forces occupying their country (see Sources 11 and 12). In 1941 General Laure, a French army officer, condemned the violence of the Maquis as 'gangsterism'. Members of the Maquis claimed to be simply defending their homes and families.

> **SOURCE 11**
>
> *Terrorist acts against the occupation authorities climbed steeply after June 1941. Colonel Hans Spiedel, Chief of Staff of the German Military Command in Paris, reported 54 acts of sabotage in July 1941, 73 in August, 134 in September and 162 in October. . . . Among them were a number of spectacular assassinations.*
>
> R. O. Paxton, Vichy France, 1972

SOURCE 12 German soldiers inspect a blown-up railway bridge in northern France, 1944.

EVENT 3

In 1933 Adolf Hitler and his Nazi Party came to power in Germany. Hitler believed that the Jews were an inferior race and planned their total extermination in a number of concentration camps (see Source 13). Rudolf Hoess was Commandant of Auschwitz concentration camp. At the end of the Second World War, at his trial, he described his work (Source 14). His defence was that he was simply obeying orders.

SOURCE 14

I was in command of Auschwitz until 1st December 1943, and estimate that at least 2,500,000 victims were liquidated [killed] there by gassing and cremation [burning]. At least a further half million died by starvation and illness, which gives a final total of approximately three million deaths. . . . When I established the liquidation chambers in Auschwitz I decided to use Zyklon-B, a crystallised prussic acid, which we injected into the gas chambers through a small opening. Depending on climatic conditions the people in the chambers generally died within 3 to 15 minutes. We knew when the occupants had died because their shouting stopped. . . . After they had been dragged out, our special commandos took the rings off the corpses and pulled out any gold teeth they might have.

SOURCE 13 Endless rows of corpses awaiting burial at Belsen concentration camp, 1945

EVENT 4

On 6th August 1945, an atomic bomb was dropped by the Americans on the Japanese city of Hiroshima (see Source 15). John Hersey, an American journalist who visited the city shortly after this event, described some of the victims (Source 16).

SOURCE 16

The eyebrows of some were burned off and skin hung from their faces and hands. Others, because of pain, held their arms up as if carrying something in both hands. Some were vomiting as they walked. Many were naked or in shreds of clothing. There were about twenty men and they were all in the same nightmarish state: their faces were wholly burned, their eyesockets were hollow, the fluid from their melted eyes had run down their cheeks. Their mouths were mere swollen, pus-covered wounds, which they could not bear to stretch enough to admit the spout of the teapot.

John Hersey, *Hiroshima*, 1946

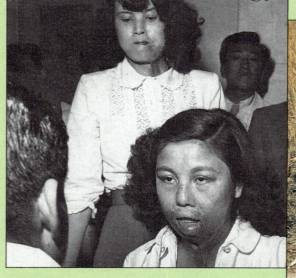

SOURCE 15 Japanese girls disfigured by burns, Hiroshima, 1945

Harry S. Truman, President of the United States of America and Commander-in-Chief of the Armed Forces, had ordered the dropping of this atomic bomb. He believed that it would save the lives of American soldiers and their allies by ending the war in the Far East.

EVENT 5

During the Vietnam War, the Communists in North Vietnam accused the American airmen and soldiers of being terrorists. Richard Brummett, who served with the American forces between July 1967 and July 1968, admitted that Vietnamese civilians had suffered at the hands of the Americans (Source 17).

In one particular incident, on 16th March 1968, C Company of the first battalion of the 20th Infantry Regiment attacked the village of My Lai in Quang Ngai Province in Vietnam. The platoon leader, Lieutenant William Calley, ordered his men to shoot the inhabitants – mainly women, children and old men. It was reported that 527 civilians were killed (see Source 18).

SOURCE 17

Incidents included random shelling of villages with 90mm white phosphorous rounds, machine gunning of civilians who had the misfortune to be near when we hit a mine, torture of prisoners, destroying of the food and livestock of the villagers if it was deemed [thought] they had an excess, and numerous burnings of villages for no apparent reasons.

R. Brummett, Letter to US Secretary of Defense, Melvin Laird, October 27th 1970

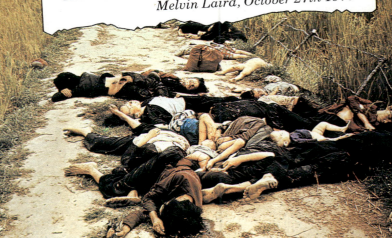

SOURCE 18 Victims of the My Lai massacre, 1968

In their defence, American soldiers pointed out that the Viet Cong (Communist forces) often disguised themselves as innocent farmers and hid in the villages.

EVENT 6

SOURCE 19 Burnt-out bus, after the massacre of Hindus, 1986

On 30th November 1986 a group of Sikh Indians ambushed a bus (see Source 19) just outside the village of Bhangol in the Punjab (a state in Northern India). Newspaper reports gave the details (see Source 20).

SOURCE 20

People still working in the fields saw a bus turn off the main road to Kashmir and head towards their village. The bus stopped suddenly near a sugar-cane field and terrified people poured out as shooting began. In less than five minutes 22 men, all Hindus except for a shaven Sikh who was taken for a Hindu, lay dead and another 8 were injured. The killers, as usual, escaped.

Sunday Times, 7th December 1986

Sikhs and Hindus hold very different religious beliefs. Sikh extremists want independence for the Punjab (where they are in the majority) from the rest of India (where Hindus are in the majority). Sikhs claim that the killings they carry out are in revenge for Hindu attacks on Sikhs.

When discussing your ideas as a class, and when you are trying to come up with an agreed class definition of a terrorist, you might like to consider the following questions:

1 Princip killed just two people. Hoess was responsible for the deaths of 3 million. Does the number of people killed determine whether or not someone is a terrorist?

2 If an act of violence is ordered by a government, does this make a difference? Can governments be guilty of terrorism?

3 Some of the events described took place in wartime. Does a state of war justify the use of unlimited violence and terror?

4 Did you find it difficult to reach a conclusion on some of these events because of lack of information? What further evidence would you have liked on each event before making up your mind?

5 All the sources in this section are either photographs or written accounts of violent acts. If you were writing a book on terrorism, what other types of historical evidence would you use?

6 If violence and terror are used in defence of your country or to protect your family and property, are they justified?

143

TERRORISM – DIFFERENT PERSPECTIVES

You may have found it difficult to decide which of the six events described in the Activity section were acts of terrorism and which were justified acts of war or self-defence. Your decisions were almost certainly influenced by your own VALUES, ATTITUDES and PREJUDICES. For example, you probably concluded that Hoess was a terrorist because he was a Nazi and it is now generally accepted that the aims of the Nazi government were evil and vicious. Truman and the Americans, on the other hand, were Britain's allies during the Second World War and so you may have justified their use of the atomic bomb against Japan.

To some extent, whether you see someone as a terrorist or not, depends on which side you are on.

In 1980 the Central Intelligence Agency of the United States produced a definition of terrorism (Source 21).

SOURCE 21

The threat or use of violence for political purposes by individuals or groups, whether acting for or in opposition to established governmental authority, when such actions are intended to shock, stun or intimidate a target group wider than the immediate victims.

Quoted in James Adams, *The Financing of Terror*, 1986

This definition is very broad. It could be used to argue that the British commandos who raided German-occupied Europe and the British airmen who bombed German cities in the Second World War were, in fact, terrorists.

In practice, the British and American governments employ a much narrower definition of terrorism. It is not simply the use of violent methods that makes a terrorist. Much more important are the aims and objectives of the people using violence. Thus individuals and groups using force against democratically elected governments are usually condemned as 'terrorists'. On the other hand, people using equal force against dictatorships or Communist governments are often seen as 'guerrillas' or 'freedom fighters'.

The British and American governments see an important difference between guerrillas and terrorists. Guerrillas, they claim, have the support of a large section of the community in which they operate and usually restrict their attacks to military targets. Terrorists, on the other hand, usually only have the support of a minority of the people they claim to represent and often wage war against innocent civilians.

This is the definition which has allowed the United States government to condemn the terrorist activities of such groups as the Palestine Liberation Front and Al Fatah while, at the same time, financing the 'guerrilla operations' of the Contras who are trying to overthrow the Communist regime in Nicaragua (see Source 22).

SOURCE 22 Contra 'guerrillas' at a training camp in Honduras. In 1986 it was revealed that members of President Reagan's Administration were selling weapons to Iran (a country known to support terrorism) and sending the profits to the Contras.

Several governments in the world are guilty of encouraging and financing different forms of terrorist activity in other states. Since he deposed King Idris of Libya in 1969, General Gaddafi has supported more than 30 terrorist groups around the world, from the Red Brigade to the IRA. Similarly, the Cuban government has trained terrorists from Nicaragua, Colombia, El Salvador, the Middle East and Angola.

> **State-backed terrorism is really just another form of warfare. It is a way of weakening a rival or enemy country without actually having to declare war on it and fight pitched battles. It is a form of warfare preferred by small, weak states against larger and stronger neighbours. Do you think state-backed terrorism can ever be justified? Explain your answer.**

The terrorists' view

The people who use violence and terror against governments and communities prefer to describe themselves as 'partisans', 'resistance workers', 'revolutionaries' or 'freedom fighters' rather than terrorists. They argue that violence is the only weapon left to them to resist the tyranny of the state.

As early as 1887 Alexander Ulyanov, the brother of the Communist revolutionary Lenin, gave an excuse for terrorism in Russia (Source 23). The Russian Tsar had been assassinated six years earlier (see Source 24).

SOURCE 24 The assassination of Tsar Alexander II, 1881

SOURCE 23

Under a system which permits no freedom of expression . . . and crushes every attempt to work for welfare and education by legal means . . . the only instrument that remains is terror. We cannot fight this regime in open battle. . . . Therefore any individual sensitive to injustice must resort to terror. Terror is our answer to the violence of the state. It is the only way to force a despotic [tyrannical] regime to grant political freedom to the people.

SOURCE 26

Terrorism should be considered a valuable tactic when it is used to put to death some noted leader of the oppressing forces well-known for his cruelty, his efficiency in repression, or any other quality that makes his elimination [removal] useful.

Thus terrorists argue that violence is justified if used against a cruel and ruthless state. If a state lives by terror, then it must die by terror. This argument may seem reasonable enough. However, much modern terrorism is not directed against cruel dictatorships but against free, democratic states. Most people find it very difficult to justify this form of terrorism.

SOURCE 25 Che Guevara, 1965

Che Guevara planned in the 1960s to spark revolution throughout Latin America (see Source 25). He provided a further defence of terrorism (Source 26).

1 Look at Source 22. The Contras are fighting the Communist government of Nicaragua. The Americans see them as freedom fighters. Why? Who might view them as terrorists? Why?

2 Do you agree with Alexander Ulyanov (Source 23) and Che Guevara (Source 26) that the use of terror against a cruel and ruthless government is justified? Explain your answer.

3 If all of these people kill, bomb and kidnap, does it matter whether they are called 'terrorists' or 'freedom fighters'? Why is the label so important?

TERRORISM IN IRELAND AND BRITAIN

8 In 1920/1921 Ireland was divided into two separate states. Northern Ireland had its government in Belfast. The Irish Free State had its government in Dublin. At first both governments were under the control of the British government in London. In 1922 the Irish Free State became independent from Britain. In 1937 it changed its name to Eire, and in 1949 it became the Republic of Ireland.

1 In 1534 King Henry VIII broke away from the Roman Catholic Church and established the Church of England. Ireland remained loyal to the Catholic Church. Fearing that their Catholic enemies abroad might attack England through Ireland, Henry VIII and his successors decided to tighten their grip on Ireland.

THE BACKGROUND TO THE TROUBLES

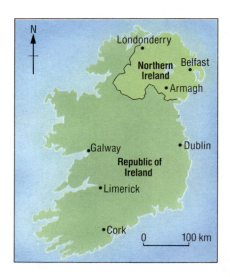

7 After the failure of the Fenian Rising in 1867, many Irishmen turned to legal methods to achieve Irish Home Rule. The Irish Home Rule Party tried to persuade MPs at Westminster to grant Ireland control over its internal affairs. Two attempts to grant Ireland some measure of Home Rule, in 1886 and 1893, were both defeated in Parliament. Many Irishmen lost faith in peaceful methods. In 1916, during the Easter Rising, Irish Nationalists seized parts of Dublin in a bid to establish their own government and achieve independence from Britain. The rising was put down by the British army, and some of the leaders were executed.

2 After the failed rebellion of 1595 to 1603, the English Crown confiscated large areas of land in the north of Ireland. Protestant Scottish and English settlers were encouraged to 'colonise' this land. They pushed the Catholic Irish to the poorer lands in the south. The Catholic Irish resented the newcomers and in 1641 rebelled. Large numbers of Protestant settlers were massacred. Oliver Cromwell's forces finally crushed the rebellion without mercy.

3 In 1689 the former Catholic king of England, James II, tried to reclaim his throne by conquering Ireland. He was defeated by the Protestant William of Orange (King William III) at the Battle of the Boyne in July 1690. This ensured the continuing dominance of the Protestant settlers in the north of Ireland. Even today Protestants in Ulster call themselves 'Orangemen'.

6 Between 1845 and 1849 a series of potato famines resulted in the death from starvation or disease of more than one million Irish. Over 780,000 Irish (mainly from the poor south) emigrated to the USA. (Today about 40 million US citizens can trace their ancestry back to Ireland.) Other southern Irish, desperate for work, moved to the richer north. The northern Protestants feared this 'Catholic invasion' and passed laws which made it difficult for Catholics to find jobs or housing.

5 In the nineteenth century largely Protestant northern Ireland enjoyed a share of the prosperity produced by the Industrial Revolution (Unit 1). New industries like shipbuilding and engineering were added to the already prosperous linen industry. Meanwhile, the mainly Catholic south remained poor and undeveloped.

4 In 1798, inspired by the American and French revolutions, some Protestants combined with the Catholics to rebel against British rule. They resented the rights and privileges reserved for members of the Church of England. The rising was defeated and in 1800 the British government passed the Act of Union which made Ireland a part of the United Kingdom. Ireland could no longer have its own separate parliament.

As the chart shows, England has been closely linked with Ireland for hundreds of years. There has frequently been bloodshed and brutality on both sides. Terrorism is not new to Ireland.

The present campaign of terror sprang from the partition of Ireland in the 1920s. Many of the Catholics who lived in Northern Ireland wanted to be reunited with their fellow-Catholics and countrymen in the Irish Free State. They felt that the Protestant majority in Northern Ireland DISCRIMINATED against them and treated them as second-class citizens.

By the 1960s the police in Northern Ireland were almost entirely Protestant. Catholics received the worst housing. Three times as many Catholics as Protestants were unemployed. Electoral boundaries were drawn up in such a way that Catholics' influence in government was kept to a minimum.

This discrimination was the result of the Protestants' own fears. The Government of Ireland Act (1920) had assumed the reunion of the two parts of Ireland some time in the future. If this happened, Protestants would find themselves at the mercy of the Catholic majority. The Protestants were afraid that this would mean the end of their own way of life. Therefore they were determined to keep their control of Northern Ireland and to maintain it as a separate country. The British government could not afford to ignore this Protestant majority.

When Catholics in Northern Ireland campaigned for equal rights they were attacked by Protestant extremists. Often the police refused to protect them. Violence increased on both sides. In August 1969 British troops were ordered into Northern Ireland to try to restore order. The British army were unable to stop the attacks against Catholics. It seemed to many Catholics that the soldiers were actually siding with the Protestants.

The British government did try to improve policing and to tackle the problems of Catholic housing and unemployment. But Catholics still felt that nothing was being done to give them a real voice in the government of Northern Ireland.

SOURCE 27 Youths confronting troops in the Bogside, Londonderry, February 1972

The Irish Republican Army

The IRA was formed in 1917. Since 1956 it has used violence to protest about the Protestant discrimination against Catholics. Its long-term aim is to force the British out of Northern Ireland and to reunite the two parts of Ireland. In 1969 the IRA split into two wings – the Provisionals and the Officials. The 'Provos' wanted to step up the campaign of violence while the Officials argued for a more peaceful solution to the problems by taking part in elections. After the split the Provos said that only they could protect the Catholic community from the Protestant extremists and the British army. They declared war on Britain and launched a campaign of bombings and assassinations in Ireland and Great Britain (see Sources 28, 30, 31 and 32).

SOURCE 30 Lord Mountbatten's funeral. He was assassinated by the IRA in August 1979.

SOURCE 31 Hyde Park car bomb, July 1982. Two Horseguardsmen and seven horses were killed.

SOURCE 28 In June 1974 an IRA bomb exploded in Westminster Hall, London, injuring 11 people.

The British government condemned the Provisional IRA as terrorists and criminals (Source 29).

SOURCE 32 Harrods car bomb, December 1983. Six people were killed.

The Provos, on the other hand, said that they were Irish soldiers fighting to free their country (Source 33).

SOURCE 34 IRA view of the 'Irish Question', from *Troops Out*.

Thus the Provos came to be seen as gangsters or heroes, depending upon which side you were on.

The Protestants were not slow to follow the lead of the Provos. They formed their own terrorist organisations, like the Ulster Defence Association (UDA) and the Ulster Freedom Fighters (UFF). Northern Ireland became the centre of a vicious circle of violence.

1 Look at Source 34. It claims that 'the agents of British rule' are the real terrorists in Northern Ireland.
   a What is meant by 'the agents of British rule'?
   b Do you think the IRA view expressed by this cartoon is reasonable?
   c Draw a similar cartoon but from a Protestant viewpoint.

2 Source 34 is taken from the pro-IRA paper *Troops Out*. 'It is obviously anti-British and is therefore useless as evidence of the causes of the troubles in Northern Ireland.' 'A historian can learn nothing of importance from it.' Explain why you agree or disagree with these statements.

3 The IRA has an estimated 300 active members, but the UDA has 50,000. Both are terrorist organisations. Why does the British government spend much more money opposing the IRA than the UDA?

The British government has spent huge sums of money opposing terrorism in Northern Ireland. In 1986, for instance, it spent £4 million a day. This policy managed to reduce the number of shootings and bombings but it failed to destroy the IRA.

One reason why the IRA continues to operate is that it receives money from Irish Americans who are sympathetic to its cause. It also gets money by running 'legal' business activities in Northern Ireland (e.g. taxi companies) and by taking part in organised crime (e.g. bank robberies). Some Catholics in Northern Ireland actively support the IRA. Others are against its tactics of violence while still wanting Northern Ireland to be reunited with the rest of Ireland. The British government refuses to give in to the demands of the IRA because a 'united Ireland' would be against the wishes of the Protestant majority in Northern Ireland. It also refuses to surrender to terrorism.

SOURCE 36 A British army patrol in a Catholic housing estate in Newry, December 1987.

SOURCE 35 In October 1984 the IRA attempted to blow up Mrs Thatcher and her Cabinet at the Grand Hotel, Brighton.

1 Look back at Source 21. Do the activities of the IRA seem to come within this definition of terrorism?

2 Look at Source 23. Could the IRA use Alexander Ulyanov's arguments to justify its use of terrorist tactics? Explain your answer carefully.

3 Now look at Source 26. Does Che Guevara's statement explain the IRA's attempt to kill Mrs Thatcher and other members of the British government (see Source 35)? Explain your answer carefully.

4 Look at Source 36. Britain is a democratic country but it has resorted to harsh measures (house-to-house searches, imprisonment without trial) to try to defeat terrorism. Do you think that here the end can be said to justify the means?

5 Drawing on the information contained in this section, including the chart, write a short paragraph about the background to the troubles from the point of view of a Northern Irish Catholic. Have there been injustices? If so, what? Before you begin you will need to decide whether you are for or against the activities of the IRA.

The future of terrorism

Although they have succeeded in causing death and destruction, most terrorist organisations have failed to achieve their objectives. Murders, kidnappings and bombings have not persuaded governments to surrender to their demands.

Many of the terrorist groups of the 1960s and 1970s — the Baader-Meinhof gang in Germany and the Japanese Red Army, for example — have disappeared. Other terrorist groups, like the IRA, have only survived because they have combined crime with legal business activities.

Recent years have seen some of Europe's leading terrorist organisations starting to work together. Western governments have been quick to respond. For example, in the Anglo–Irish Treaty (1985) the British and Irish governments agreed to work together against terrorism by sharing information and by improving security along the border. This increasing co-operation between governments is probably the best hope of containing terrorism in the future. But terrorism can only be defeated when the flow of money that feeds it has finally been stopped.

ASSESSMENT

Empathy

1 In 1970 the British government gave in to the demands of the PFLP and released Leila Khaled.
   a Make two lists showing the arguments *for* and *against* this decision.
   b What action would you have taken if you had been the British Prime Minister at the time?

Change

2 The use of force has often changed the course of history. Obvious examples drawn from this book are the French Revolution of 1789, the Russian Revolution of 1917, the First World War (1914–1918), and the Second World War (1939–1945). You can probably think of other occasions in the past when violence has produced important changes.
   a Make a list of all the changes produced by violence which you can think of.
   b Now write your list out again in two columns. In one column put those changes where you think the use of violence was right and justified, and in the other put those changes where you think it was wrong and unjustified.
   c Explain how you reached your decisions. When is the use of violence justified? Which ends, if any, may justify violent means?

Empathy

3 Work in pairs. Consider the following 'labels' (look up any you are unsure about in a dictionary): *gunman, hero, nationalist, agitator, anarchist, insurgent, freedom fighter, revolutionary, resistance worker, guerrilla, militant, rebel, radical, dissident, partisan, liberator.* If you were involved in terrorist activities, which labels might you use to describe yourself? Which would you be unlikely to use?

Cross-reference

4 Gandhi's whole purpose was to achieve change through non-violence (Unit 8). Terrorists aim to achieve change through violence. Compare, in a class discussion, the success of terrorists, using violence, with the achievements of Gandhi, using non-violence. Which method seems more effective?

To discuss

Some people think that detailed TV and newspaper coverage of terrorist activities like bombings, assassinations and kidnappings encourages terrorism. Do you agree with this view?

TIMELINE

DATE	LEADERS	POLITICAL EVENTS	SOCIAL AND ECONOMIC EVENTS
1750			
1775		1776 American War of Independence	1769 Arkwright's water frame 1771 Cromford Mill built
1800	1793 Louis XVI executed	1789 French Revolution begins 1792 French Revolutionary Wars begin	
1825			
1850		1857–1947 India governed by British Crown	1834 Tolpuddle Martyrs 1845–1858 Irish Potato Famine 1840s and 1850s Peak decades of Irish migration to Britain
1875	1881 Tsar Alexander assassinated	1870 War between France and Germany 1871 German Empire set up	1871 Trade Disputes Act
1900		1914–1918 First World War 1916 Easter Rising in Dublin 1917 Bolshevik Revolution in Russia 1918–1920 Russian Civil War 1918–1933 Weimar Republic in Germany	1890s–1914 Suffragette activities 1897 Workmen's Compensation Act 1918 Votes for women (over 30) in Britain
1925	1918 German Kaiser abdicates 1919 Gandhi becomes active in India 1933 Roosevelt becomes President of USA 1933 Hitler becomes German Chancellor 1948 Gandhi assassinated 1949 Mao Zedong becomes leader of China	1919 Treaty of Versailles 1923 Nazi revolt in Munich 1939–1945 Second World War 1945 USA drops atom bombs on Hiroshima and Nagasaki 1947 India and Pakistan achieve independence 1948 Berlin Blockade 1949 NATO formed 1949 East and West Germany formed	1923 High inflation in Germany 1928 Votes for women (over 21) in Britain 1933 New Deal begins in USA 1948 British Nationalities Act
1950			
1975	1979 Margaret Thatcher becomes British Prime Minister 1985 Gorbachev becomes leader of USSR	1961 Berlin Wall built 1962 Cuban missile crisis 1965 USA enters Vietnam War 1969 British troops sent to Northern Ireland 1970 'Skyjack Sunday' 1971 Bangladesh formed 1979 Soviet invasion of Afghanistan 1982 Falklands War 1985 Anglo-Irish Treaty	1960s Women's Liberation movements formed in Britain 1960s–1970s Bengali immigration to Britain 1975 Sex Discrimination Act 1976 Race Relations Act
2000			

LOCATION MAP

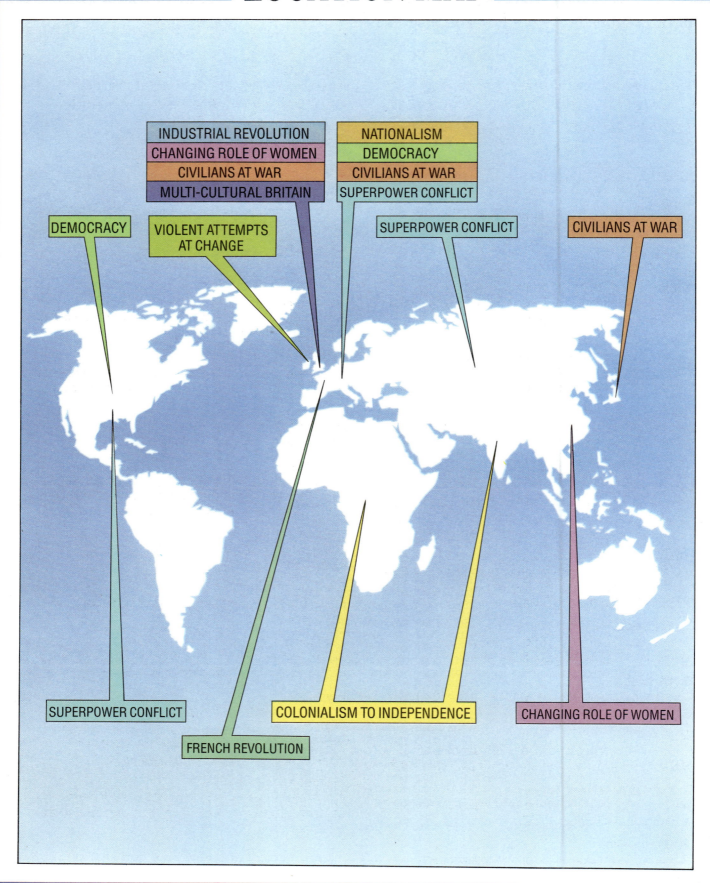

INDUSTRIAL REVOLUTION
CHANGING ROLE OF WOMEN
CIVILIANS AT WAR
MULTI-CULTURAL BRITAIN

NATIONALISM
DEMOCRACY
CIVILIANS AT WAR
SUPERPOWER CONFLICT

DEMOCRACY

VIOLENT ATTEMPTS
AT CHANGE

SUPERPOWER CONFLICT

CIVILIANS AT WAR

SUPERPOWER CONFLICT

COLONIALISM TO INDEPENDENCE

CHANGING ROLE OF WOMEN

FRENCH REVOLUTION

GLOSSARY

Abdication
Resignation of an emperor, king or queen.

Attitudes
Ways of thinking and feeling about something or somebody.

Black marketeers
People who trade illegally in goods in short supply.

Budget
A government's annual estimate of its income and expenditure.

Capitalist
A person or country that supports an economic and political system in which property, business and industry are owned by private individuals and are run in competition with each other for profit.

Censor
To examine plays, books, letters, newspapers, etc. and cut out any parts of them that are immoral, reveal military secrets or damage the country's reputation.

Colonialism
The practice by which a powerful country controls less powerful countries and uses their resources in order to increase its own wealth and power.

Communist
A person or country that believes that the state should own and control the means of producing everything so that all levels of society can be made equal.

Congress
The elected group of politicians that is responsible for making the law in the USA. It consists of the House of Representatives and the Senate.

Constituency
A town or area which is officially allowed to elect someone to represent them in Parliament.

Constitution
A system of laws and rules which formally states people's rights and duties.

Continuity
The smooth development and continuation of a process, system or way of life over a period of time.

Convention
The assembly which replaced the Legislative Assembly in France in September 1792.

Decolonisation
The process of colonies becoming independent.

Defeatists
People who think or talk in a way that suggests that they expect to fail or be defeated (in war time).

Depression, The
The decline in many countries' industries and economies in the 1930s which caused much unemployment and poverty.

Democratic government
Government which consists of representatives who have been elected by the people.

Deterrent
A weapon to discourage enemies from attacking by making them afraid to do so.

Dictatorship
A form of government where all power rests with an individual or a political group.

Discrimination
The practice of treating one person or group of people less fairly or less well than another person or group of people.

Diversity
Variety; range of difference.

Empathy
The ability to understand (though not necessarily to share) another person's emotions, feelings, attitudes and experiences as if they were your own.

Evacuation
The movement of people to a place of safety from an area of danger.

Evolution
The process of gradual change that takes place over many years.

Exploited
Treated or used unfairly, often by a person or group of people who are only interested in making money.

Fascism
A right-wing political idea that believes in having a powerful dictator and state control of all aspects of society and the economy. Nationalistic feelings are encouraged and political opposition is forbidden.

Flashpoint
A place which people think is dangerous because political trouble may start there and then spread to other areas.

Gestapo
Geheime Staatspolizei; the state secret police run by Hitler and his Nazi Party.

Ideologies
The political beliefs on which people, parties and countries base their actions.

Immigration
The coming of people into a country in order to live and work there.

Independence
Self-government; freedom from control by another country or other countries.

Inflation
A general increase in the price of goods and services in a country.

Jingoism
An unreasonable belief in the superiority of your own country, especially when it involves support for a war against another country.

Legislature
The group of people in a country who have the power to make and pass laws.

Mass production
The manufacture of goods on a large scale, using machines in factories.

Morale
The amount of confidence or optimism a person feels in a difficult, dangerous or important situation.

National Front
A right-wing British political organisation which believes in nationalism, racism and the use of threats and violence.

Nationalism
1 Love of your nation which often amounts to a feeling that your nation is better than any other.
2 A desire for the political independence of your nation.

Neo-colonialism
The economic or political influence that one country has over another country that is in theory independent.

Non-aligned
A country that does not support and is not a member of any organisation led by either USA or USSR.

Nuclear
Using the energy released by atoms.

Patent
An official right to be the only person or company allowed to make or sell a new product for a certain period of time.

Persecution
Cruel or unfair treatment of a person or group especially because of their religious or political beliefs.

Perspective
A particular way of thinking about or viewing something.

Police State
A country where the government controls people's freedom by means of the police, especially secret police.

Prejudice
An unreasonable dislike of or preference for something.

Propaganda
Exaggerated or false information circulated to influence people's opinions.

Racism
The treatment of some people as inferior because they belong to a particular race.

Radiation
Radioactive waves or very small particles, produced for example by nuclear weapons, that can cause illness and death if your body is exposed to them.

Reformers
People who try to improve something, such as a law or social system.

Religious persecution
The cruel and unfair treatment of people because of their religious beliefs.

Representative
Person who has been chosen by another person or group of people to act or make decisions on their behalf.

Revolution
1 A successful attempt by a large group of people, often using violent methods, to change the political and social systems of their country.
2 An important change in a particular kind of human activity, such as the way things are made.

Speculators
People who hope to make a great deal of money quickly in risky commercial deals.

Stormtroopers

Stürmabteilung; the private army of the Nazi Party. They wore brown shirts and jackboots and used threats and violence against their political opponents.

Tyranny

Harsh, unjust government by one or more persons (tyrants).

Values

The principles and beliefs that people think are important and guide their actions.

Veto

The power to prohibit some action proposed by others, or the use of that power.

Viceroy

The person ruling a colony on behalf of their king or queen.

Most of these definitions have been taken from or adapted from the *Collins Cobuild English Language Dictionary*.

SKILLS GRID

This grid tells you what you will learn to do in each unit in this book.

	Historical Ideas	Ways of Understanding History				
		Role of the individual	Cause and consequence	Similarity and difference	Change	Continuity
UNIT 1 **The Industrial Revolution**	Industrialisation Urbanisation Reform				✓	✓
UNIT 2 **The French Revolution**	Revolution Divided society Tyranny	✓	✓			
UNIT 3 **The Changing Role of Women**	Rights Discrimination Reform	✓		✓	✓	
UNIT 4 **Nationalism**	Nationalism Dictatorship Totalitarianism	✓	✓			
UNIT 5 **Democracy**	Democracy Dictatorship			✓	✓	
UNIT 6 **Civilians at War**	Military technology Morale Total War				✓	
UNIT 7 **Superpower Conflict**	Ideologies Propaganda Cold war			✓		
UNIT 8 **Colonialism to Independence**	Colonialism Independence Empire	✓	✓			
UNIT 9 **Multi-cultural Britain**	Migration Prejudice Immigration Racism		✓	✓		✓
UNIT 10 **Violent Attempts at Change**	Terrorism Sectarianism				✓	

Evidence Skills						Empathy	
Comprehension	Primary and secondary sources	Inference	Bias and reliability	Utility	Cross-reference		
		✓	✓		✓	✓	UNIT 1
						✓	UNIT 2
				✓			UNIT 3
						✓	UNIT 4
						✓	UNIT 5
✓	✓			✓		✓	UNIT 6
✓		✓	✓				UNIT 7
				✓			UNIT 8
					✓		UNIT 9
			✓		✓	✓	UNIT 10

ACKNOWLEDGEMENTS

The publishers would like to thank the following for permission to reproduce photographs (the page number is followed, where necessary, by: t-top, b-bottom, r-right, l-left, m-middle):
Mike Abrahams/Network 136; Katalin Arkell/Network 132, 134; John Arthur/Reflex 150t; Associated Press 67bl, 139; Barnabys Picture Library 11, 112r; BBC Hulton Picture Library 15, 17, 19t, 19m, 20, 24, 37t, 40t, 84t, 84b (and cover), 108t, 109tl, 109tr, 112m, 113, 125(6), 125(10), 125(11), 145t; Bildarchiv Preussischer Kulturbesitz 57, 78t, 102; Bridgeman Art Library 27, 28; British Museum 124(5); Bundesarchiv, FRG 54b; Camera Press 37b, 48, 49, 53, 60, 79l, 86, 91, 117, 122, 141b, 148l, 148t; J Allan Cash 65, 67r; Colorific 142r, 144; Columbia Pictures 104, 115, 116; Edimedia 34; ET Archives 41l, 58, 109b (and cover); Mary Evans Picture Library 7, 9b, 13t, 14t, 22, 36, 39l, 42b, 43b, 108b, 125(7), 126, 127, 129, 130, 140; Gina Glover/Photo Co-op 39r; Sally and Richard Greenhill 40b, 44, 45r, 46, 47; Robert Hunt 56t, 56b, 83, 85, 93b, 101, 142l; Illustrated London News 81t, 128; Keystone 75l, 78b, 124(12); Leeds Central Library 6; Library of Congress 93t; Mansell Collection 18,

19b, 26, 105, 106, 110, 111, 124(4), 125(8); Museum in the Docklands 133; National Portrait Gallery 9t; Peter Newark 72b; Popperfoto 56m, 64t, 68, 70r, 72t, 79r, 112l, 138 (and cover), 145b; Museo del Prado, Madrid 82; Rex Features 38b, 62, 67t, 90, 143, 148br, 149, 150b; Ann Ronan 8, 13b, 38t; Ronald Sheridan 124(1); Liz Somerville 135; David Taylor 42t; Topham 41r, 45l, 54t, 64b, 69t, 75r, 76, 81b, 99b, 118, 119, 141t, 147; Roger Viollet 32; Vision International 43t.
The authors and publishers also wish to thank the following for permission to reproduce copyright material: Hamish Hamilton for the extract from *When the Wind Blows*; *The Times* for the extracts on pages 138 and 139; *Punch* for the extract on page 63.

Every effort has been made to contact owners of copyright material but if any have been inadvertently overlooked the publishers will be pleased to make the necessary arrangements at the first opportunity.

Collins Educational, 8 Grafton Street, London W1X 3LA

© Peter Fisher and Nicholas Williams
First published 1989
ISBN 0 00 327222 2

Designed by Glynis Edwards

Artwork by Jerry Collins, Douglas Williamson

Typeset by CG Graphic Services, Tring

Printed and bound by G. Canale & C. s.p.a., Italy